The Railways of Northern England
IN THE 1960s

MICHAEL CLEMENS

First published in Great Britain in 2025 by
Fonthill
An imprint of
Pen & Sword Books Ltd
Yorkshire – Philadelphia
www.fonthill.media

Copyright © Michael Clemens 2025

ISBN 978-1-78155-911-6

The right of Michael Clemens to be identified as Author of this work has been asserted by him in accordance with the Copyright, Designs and Patents Act 1988.
A CIP catalogue record for this book is
available from the British Library.

All rights reserved. No part of this book may be reproduced or transmitted in any form or by any means, electronic or mechanical including photocopying, recording or by any information storage and retrieval system, without permission from the Publisher in writing.

The Publisher's authorised representative in the EU for product safety is Authorised Rep Compliance Ltd., Ground Floor,
71 Lower Baggot Street, Dublin D02 P593, Ireland.
www.arccompliance.com

For a complete list of Pen & Sword titles please contact
PEN & SWORD BOOKS LIMITED
47 Church Street, Barnsley, South Yorkshire, S70 2AS, England
E-mail: enquiries@pen-and-sword.co.uk
Website: www.pen-and-sword.co.uk

Or
PEN AND SWORD BOOKS
1950 Lawrence Rd, Havertown, PA 19083, USA
E-mail: Uspen-and-sword@casematepublishers.com
Website: www.penandswordbooks.com

Introduction

For those who have read my previous books, this latest follows a similar format; however, for the benefit of those who have not, a brief recap of how this archive was created follows. My father, C. N. 'Jim' Clemens (1922–1987), set out to record the railways of Britain and the steam locomotives that worked over them when the network was still largely intact, and as long as it was not during term-time at school, I would also generally be there using still and ciné cameras plus also making tape recordings (I was born in August 1951). Nevertheless, let me make it very clear, the credit for creating the archive lies with my father, although what I do not think he realised at the time is the tremendous interest nowadays (some fifty or sixty years after the photographs in this book were taken) in old railways and nostalgia generally.

This is my fifteenth railway photobook and the time period covered is approximately the fifteen years or so from the mid-1950s until the early 1970s. The most significant feature of this book compared to others about the railways of the North of England is the photographs. While little of the written detail will probably be new, virtually all of the photographs—a glorious combination of colour and black and white—have never been published before. Steam is naturally very well represented with BR and industrial examples, but as is electric (BR and, perhaps surprisingly, industrial), plus there are some early BR diesels such as the 'Deltics' and the later Class 40s; there are even examples of cable-worked inclines (powered and gravity). It will appeal to railway enthusiasts, modellers, and those with an interest in local history.

The Railways of Northern England in the 1960s is almost entirely made up from photographs taken by my late father and me, with some additions from two of my father's old pals and my school friend; sadly, all have now passed on. Sometimes my father's friends would accompany us, but others date from their own independent visits, and I have been very fortunate in being allowed to use their material in this book. You will see the names of Ellis James-Robertson (1922–2015) and Alan Maund (1930–1983) mentioned in various photographic credits; their excellent material included thanks to the permission of their daughters/widow. Eric Parker (1900–1988) was a great stickler for the written record, and his diaries given to me by his daughter, Valerie, have been a priceless source of information in compiling some of the commentaries.

Finally, there are some photographs taken by my friend from Prince Henry's Grammar School, Evesham—Michael Bailey. I was very lucky throughout my school years and was able to use my father's equipment, but this option was not open to Michael. Instead, he used his own Kodak 'Instamatic'—an easy-to-use and relatively inexpensive 'point and shoot' type of camera. They used 126 film in a cartridge (so no having to manually load and thread each reel) that produced a square image instead of oblong with 35-mm, but (using today's terminology) with less 'pixels'. We both travelled on a number of the Worcester Locomotive Society (WLS) 'shed bash' tours involving early departures from home and late arrivals back; all of Michael Bailey's photographs were taken during WLS shed visits. For those interested in the locomotives seen during these shed visits, click on michaelclemensrailways.co.uk and then 'Michael Bailey Photo Archive'; Michael's trainspotting notes from the time can be downloaded here. Sadly, Michael died very unexpectedly in June 2018; he was born during June 1951.

It was Cornish-born engineer and inventor Richard Trevithick (1771–1833) who built the steam engine used for the world's first locomotive-hauled railway journey in 1804, along the Penydarren Tramway near Merthyr Tydfil in South Wales. But it was around the North of England where much pioneering development took place and names have earned their place in the history of railways and steam locomotives, such as George Stephenson, the Stockton & Darlington Railway, and the Liverpool & Manchester Railway. There was still the odd connection to be seen from the early days at the time of our visits and amazingly, it was still possible to see railway operations whose origins dated from a previous era using gravity and stationary engines.

Until the spring of 1966 most of our colour photographs were taken with a German Super Baldina 35-mm camera, a Minolta SR1 (that I still have) was then purchased for this type of work; the colour film used was mainly Agfa CT18 with some Kodachrome II. For black & white work a modest Halina 35X camera was used with either Ilford HP3 film or, for a short time during 1966–67, Gaevert Dia-Direct transparencies. I have no knowledge of the camera used by Alan Maund but Ellis James-Robertson used tip-top equipment (a Rolleiflex twin lens camera with 120 roll film) for his monochrome images in this book; he was also a member of the Guild of Railway Artists, this probably part-explaining the stunning images that he took.

In very broad terms, the area covered in this book is that north of a line linking Chester, Crewe, Sheffield, Doncaster, and the Humber, all the way up to approaching the border with Scotland at Carlisle and Tweedmouth. More specifically, it begins at Crewe with 'Coronations' at the station, plus a visit to the works that includes a brand-new diesel, a Lancashire & Yorkshire Railway works shunter, plus a Victorian steam tramway locomotive. Next is a visit to Birkenhead shed and Woodside station before crossing the Mersey to Edge Hill shed where a couple of ex-Crostis languish in the snow.

Warrington Bank Quay station is seen during 1959 as an ex-Midland Railway 3F passes through; also included is a visit to nearby Dallam engine shed some eight years later. The North of England has a proud industrial heritage and a number of visits are made to National Coal Board (NCB) collieries. First is Bickershaw with the 'newest' of all the photographs in this book, where steam was still operating commercially in 1976. Northwich follows on a foggy winter's day in early 1968 interspersed with sleet showers, but Gorton works are seen during mid-summer 1960 including an ex-works EM1 Bo+Bo in colour. Other locations in the North-West include: Stockport Edgeley shed, Rose Grove shed, and Preston. Class 502 EMUs are seen on the line from Liverpool to Southport before one of the ex-LNWR First World War-era units at Morecambe that were refitted as prototype AM1 AC EMUs.

The Clemens family holidays always seemed to involve some kind of railway theme and the summer of 1964 was no exception with a fortnight on the Isle of Man. The Isle of Man Railway system was still largely operating the way it had for decades, before its closedown at the end of 1965; it then restarted in 1967 at the beginning of the 'Ailsa' era. Steam predominates, but also included are the ex-County Donegal railcars, and visits are made to the impressive station at Douglas, plus Port Erin, Peel, and Foxdale. The Manx Electric and the Snaefell Mountain railways are also covered.

Alan Maund visited Oxenholme station in the summer of 1963 and included here is one of the visibly different Stanier 8Fs with a larger than usual War Department-type top feed. When driving to Scotland from Worcestershire, my father would stop for a while just to the north of Shap Summit and among the locomotives seen during Easter 1963 was 'Patriot' No. 45522 *Prestatyn* storming up the grade. Visits were also undertaken to industrial sites in Cumbria—Haig Colliery, the Corkickle Brake cable-worked incline, and Solway Colliery at Whitehaven.

Journeys are made in 1955 and 1961 across the Pennines over the Stainmore route that closed in January 1962: Barnard Castle, Barras, Belah and Deepdale viaducts, Kirkby Stephen East, Tebay, and Penrith. Eerie Bowes station is seen a few years after closure and looks like the set of a horror movie, and then onwards to Carlisle, which also includes a visit to Kingmoor shed.

Doncaster works and shed are seen in 1959 and 1964, and then something a bit different: the coal-fired paddle steamer, PS *Lincoln Castle*, plying its trade across the Humber. The last city tramway system in the country at Sheffield is studied during August 1960 and just before closure in the October. Then forwards via Wakefield, the 'Harrogate Sunday Pullman' is seen at Leeds, and on to York, and included here is something that always arouses the interest of enthusiasts: a 9F working a passenger service in 1960. On the way, stops are made at a number of NCB sites: South Kirkby, Water Haigh, and Peckfield. From York, the journey continues via Market Weighton, Bridlington, Filey Holiday Camp (Butlin's), Scarborough, and Malton.

Many of the next two dozen or so photographs were taken by Ellis James-Robertson, and in among them are some of his stunning black and white images using a Rolleiflex twin-lens camera and 120 roll film as we travel on via Kirbymoorside, a lovely colour study at Tadcaster, then Hammerton, Brafferton, Alne, Pilmoor, Sessay, Thirsk, Otterington, Melmerby, and Sinderby, before spending time at Northallerton.

The old Catterick Camp Military Railway is seen in 1960 before arrival at Darlington in 1963 where we get our first glimpse of a 'Deltic', Wrexham-allocated No. 75006 is under repair at the works in 1964 and a very long way from its Welsh home. Still in use at Seaham were wooden-framed chaldron wagons that had their origins hundreds of years earlier. At Sunderland, visits are made to Ryhope Junction, South Dock shed, Wearmouth Colliery, and the famous Doxford's shipyard with their delightful crane tanks. A feature at Sunderland and other north-eastern depots towards the end of steam compared with the rest of the country was the number of Pre-Grouping-designed locomotives still active; the BR total on 1 January 1967 was fifty-one, of which forty were in the north-east.

What might have appeared to be a relic from times past was in fact a highly capable system efficiently transporting large quantities of coal—the Bowes Railway. This incorporated a number of cable-worked inclines (gravity and powered), plus some rather dangerous-looking operating practices well before the era of Health & Safety assessments. By the time of these photographs, the coal industry in the west of County Durham was being largely abandoned, future prospects were in the east drawing on under-sea reserves. The coal carrying Harton Railway at South Shields was one such example and the total antithesis of things seemingly old fashioned and dirty; it was powered by electricity and used white locomotives.

Shed visits are made to Tyne Dock and Gateshead before a 'Deltic' in pristine condition less than two months old is seen heading north from Newcastle in 1961. My father travelled on the 'Wansbeck Wanderer' rail tour from Newcastle to Rothbury, then Whittle Colliery is visited, and finally the border with Scotland is reached at Tweedmouth and Coldstream. *The Railways of Northern England in the 1960s* concludes with a delightful view of something that was rare even when the photograph was taken in 1960: a 1926-built Foden Steam Wagon that had been converted into a tar sprayer, working close to the A1 south of Catterick.

Finally, I would like to thank various societies and individuals who have freely given me their help in the making of this book: Severn Valley Railway Association (Stourbridge Branch); Chipping Norton Railway Club; Amanda Cuskin (Outreach Learning and Volunteer Support Officer) at the Bowes Railway Museum; John Harkness, a one-time engine driver at Harrington Colliery, Lowca; and Peter Burgess and his website (www.cumbria-railways.co.uk).

Michael Clemens,
Pershore, Worcestershire
December 2024

By July 1963, the summertime-only 'Lakes Express' was one of the few named express services still regularly hauled by Stanier's 'Coronation' pacifics; an unidentified example heads towards Crewe just to the south of Hartford. (*Alan Maund*)

One for the locomotive experts: during September 1967, Carlisle Kingmoor-allocated 'Britannia' No. 70032 *Tennyson* is just to the west of Crewe South engine shed and coupled to the wrong sort of tender; it has a full-width BR1D example instead of an inset coal space type BR1.

The now-preserved 9F 2-10-0 No. 92203 stands at Birkenhead Woodside on 5 March 1967 ready to work the Stephenson Locomotive Society's (Midland Area) 'Farewell to the GWR Birmingham to Birkenhead Service' rail tour to Chester and back.

The Worcester Locomotive Society organised their 'Thirteen depots in the Chester area, plus Crewe works' coach tour on 29 October 1967; this is Birkenhead shed with Caprotti valve gear No. 73135 and taken with a Kodak 'Instamatic' camera. (*Michael Bailey*)

Above: It was still possible to seek out steam locomotives working commercially well into the 1970s; Giesl ejector-equipped 'Austerity' 0-6-0ST *Respite* is at Bickershaw Colliery to the south-east of Wigan during April 1976.

Right: Well-presented 'Black 5' No. 45104 stands at Bolton shed (9K) on 12 February 1968; there were still 151 'Black 5s' in service at the very end of 1967 out of a total BR steam stock of 362 (including three narrow-gauge examples).

The delightful-sounding Rose Grove was of one of the last three BR main line depots to remain open for steam. This view was taken on Sunday, 28 July 1968; it closed the following Sunday.

Another Worcester Locomotive Society coach tour, this time 'Twelve depots in Manchester area' on 16 July 1967: Nos 73039 and 45421 simmer away on Lostock Hall shed, Preston; this was also one of the very last BR main line steam depots. (*Michael Bailey*)

Right: The Clemens summer family holiday in 1964 was two weeks at Douglas on the Isle of Man. This is the author's Isle of Man Railway, child 'Holiday Runabout Ticket'.

Below: It is Maundy Thursday, 7 April 1966, and we enjoyed a steam-hauled journey from Crewe to Carlisle on a relief to the 'Mid-day Scot'. 'Britannia' No. 70031 *Byron* climbs the Northern Fells just to the south of Oxenholme.

Above: The north end of Penrith for Ullswater station on 17 August 1961. Ellis has listed this photograph as 'No. 46120 passes "Stanier Pacific" at 12.50 p.m.' (*Ellis James-Robertson*)

Below: On 30 August 1959, our friend Alan Maund travelled on an SLS tour hauled by Midland Railway 'Compound' No. 1000 that included a visit to here at Doncaster. This is A2/2 No. 60502 *Earl Marischal*, a rebuild of one of Gresley's P2 2-8-2s; note the Kylchap exhaust assembly inside the smokebox. (*Alan Maund*)

Right: Almost anything using coal and steam would be recorded and this smoky photograph is of PS *Lincoln Castle*. Built on the Clyde at the beginning of the Second World War, this triple expansion paddle steamer (PS) was used for the ferry service across the Humber between New Holland and Hull.

Below: The last city tramway in England was that at Sheffield, and the final route to remain open was shut down on Saturday, 8 October 1960. This view along Pinstone Street of post-war car No. 517 was taken on 10 August 1960. (*Ellis James-Robertson*)

'Peak' class diesel D88 is at Leeds City station on Sunday, 8 October 1961, with enthusiasts and staff looking on. This locomotive had entered service during March 1961 and now awaits custom with inter-regional service 1V47, a through train to Bristol that Ellis James-Robertson will use to get back home to Worcester. (*Ellis James-Robertson*)

There are some excellent photographs north of York on the 'racing ground' from Darlington and this is looking south at Alne on 16 August 1960 where the track had recently been quadrupled. An unidentified V2 has a train of four- and six-wheeled Guinness road tankers on six-wheeled rail chassis. (*Ellis James-Robertson*)

March-allocated V2 No. 60803 heads a coal train south at Thirsk by the A61 road bridge on 11 August 1960 at 12.47 p.m. (*Ellis James-Robertson*)

Shadows are lengthening and there are stooks in the field on the evening of 10 August 1960. This panorama is taken from the road bridge to the north of the 1958-closed station at Otterington; D253 races past with a Newcastle to Liverpool express. (*Ellis James-Robertson*)

D3313 has charge of the branch freight train to Masham from Melmerby at Wath gates crossing on 15 August 1960; this branch had lost its passenger service nearly thirty years previously. (*Ellis James-Robertson*)

K1 No. 62005 stands at Filey Holiday Camp station with the 'Whitby Moors' rail tour on Saturday, 6 March 1965; it had opened in 1947 serving the Butlin's holiday camp here.

The Hawthorne Combined Coal Mine to the south of Sunderland was officially opened at the beginning of January 1960 and is seen during March 1970; this mine holds the European record for production in one day from one shaft—some 12,000 tons.

The north-east of England was famous in the latter days of steam for the number of Pre-Grouping-designed locomotives still at work in the area. This is Ryhope Junction, Sunderland, as the now-preserved J27 No. 65894 catches the evening sun during March 1967.

Left: A lovely selection of signals photographed close to Tyne Dock engine shed in March 1967; the signal box in the middle distance is Tyne Dock Bank Top.

Below: The 'Wansbeck Wanderer' rail tour is at Rothbury as Darlington-allocated No. 43129 runs round on Saturday, 9 November 1963; freight services ceased this weekend although regular passenger services had finished some eleven years previously.

The Railways of Northern England
IN THE 1960s

Crewe station is seen on two separate occasions. First, at the north end, No. 46251 *City of Nottingham* has charge of the Railway Correspondence & Travel Society's (RCTS) 'Duchess Commemorative' rail tour on 5 October 1963, the author's child ticket included. It would haul this return journey to Edinburgh Princes Street throughout and on the way back ran the 32.2 miles from Tebay to Lancaster (pass to pass) in twenty-four minutes and three seconds at an average speed above 80 mph—believed an all-time record for steam. Secondly, at the southern end, No. 46256 *Sir William A. Stanier F.R.S.* is taking out a London-bound service exactly one month earlier on 5 September 1963.

The Stephenson Locomotive Society (SLS) ran their 'Midland Compound 1000 Special' rail tour on 26 June 1960 directly inside the Crewe works complex to Stone Yard Bank, allowing participants to enjoy about 100 minutes exploring the facility. Standing outside the paint shop is newly-constructed D5085; this locomotive was later renumbered to No. 24085 and withdrawn in 1976. 'Princess Royal' No. 46211 *Queen Maud* seems to have been a frequent visitor to Crewe works in 1960 as four occasions are listed between January and October. The livery is Brunswick green with orange and black lining that was first applied in 1952; *Queen Maud* was withdrawn in October 1961. (*Ellis James-Robertson*)

Above and opposite page: All these three photographs were taken either in or around the environs of Crewe works on 26 June 1960. Early passenger tramways used horses as the motive power, the law preventing steam traction from operating on public highways until the end of the 1870s. This change created something of a boom in steam-powered tramways during the 1880s, a decade in which no fewer than forty-five such tramways were opened. One such was the Manchester, Bury, Rochdale & Oldham Tramway that, when completed in 1884, was the largest steam tramway operation in the world; it totalled 33¼ miles despite never actually reaching Manchester. The first photograph shows MBR&OT No. 84, one of a batch of four vertical boiler locomotives ordered by the company from Beyer, Peacock in 1886. Its tramway working life was spent operating between Rochdale and Oldham until 1904 when it was sold for £50 to the Ince Forge Company of Wigan along with two others. No. 84 remained active at Wigan until February 1954 and was the last survivor of the three. Its historical significance was recognised and No. 84 was presented to the British Transport Commission. It was initially stored at Crewe plus a number of other locations later, but is now at the National Tramway Museum, Crich in an un-restored and dismantled condition. Secondly, one of the Crewe works shunters on this day was No. 52459. This class of 0-6-0 was the Lancashire & Yorkshire Railway's standard freight locomotive and 484 of these Class 27s were built from 1889–1918. Constructed at the L&YR's Horwich works in 1909, No. 52459 transferred from Rose Grove to Crewe works in 1953 and was withdrawn at the end of 1961. Finally, a view inside the works themselves includes 8F No. 48612 nearest to the camera. (*Ellis James-Robertson*)

24

Above and opposite page: Birkenhead shed was one of the last BR depots to have a substantial allocation of steam locomotives. At the beginning of January 1967, seventy locomotives were allocated here; this was the second-highest allocation anywhere in the country, and only Carlisle Kingmoor had more with 129. As steam was run down and depots closed, more and more of the 9F 2-10-0s were transferred to Birkenhead; there were fifty-nine allocated here in early 1967. The author's father and friend, Eric Parker, visited on Thursday, 9 February 1967, and thanks to Eric's diaries, I have a record of their visit to this very grimy-looking depot. Forty-five locomotives were on shed; twenty-nine were 9Fs (including one ex-Crosti, No. 92020), two 8Fs, five 'Jintys', five 'Crabs', and four 2-6-4Ts (see also page 8). The first two photographs were taken at Birkenhead shed during their visit. The depot was also famous as being the final home of the 'Crab' 2-6-0s with their large, steeply inclined outside cylinders. The last two 'Crabs', including No. 42727 seen here, had been withdrawn in January 1967. The final photograph shows the impressive terminus of Birkenhead Woodside on the last day of through services from London Paddington, Sunday, 5 March 1967 (see also page 8). It had two semi-cylindrical overall roofs and was notable for its good light and airiness. The station had opened in 1878, was joint LNWR and GWR, and was close by the landing stages. Importantly for the GWR, this was how the company reached the prize of Liverpool, or at least just a ferry journey away across the Mersey from that city. Birkenhead-allocated Stanier 2-6-4T No. 42616 was acting as station pilot and is standing on one of the station's middle lines. Following cessation of the through London Paddington trains (that also included an overnight sleeper) an hourly DMU service to Chester and trains to Helsby continued for some eight months before total closure and then demolition. No. 42616 survived to be inter-regionally transferred to Low Moor (Bradford) and was withdrawn from there in early October 1967.

Above and opposite page: Two photographs taken by the author's late school friend, Michael Bailey, on his Kodak Instamatic camera during a Worcester Locomotive Society trip listed as 'Eleven Depots in the Crewe Area' on 10 December 1967. This is Edge Hill shed, Liverpool, and Michael has listed the two ex-Crostis as Nos 92021 and 92029. Both had been allocated to Birkenhead but were withdrawn on its closure to steam the month previously. Presumably, that furthest from the camera is No. 92021, as this ran with a BR1G inset tender from 1965 until withdrawal, instead of the more usual full-width type. Steam working from Edge Hill ceased during May 1968. (*Michael Bailey*)

Above and opposite page: The first two photographs at Warrington Dallam shed were taken during the early evening of Thursday, 20 July 1967. This ten-track brick-built dead-ended depot was to the west of the West Coast Main Line (WCML) and north of Warrington Bank Quay station. The shed had been opened in 1888 by the LNWR and replaced an earlier facility that had become inadequate due to increasing traffic. The bridge in the left background, which no longer exists, carried the Cheshire Lines Committee tracks that avoided Warrington Central station. Things did not go well here for my father's party (the author was at school on this day); they were ordered off the premises and had to content themselves with photography from the Folly Lane road bridge. Prominent is No. 73144, one of the BR Standard Class 5s with Caprotti valve gear allocated to Patricroft, Manchester, and the 9F is believed to be No. 92152 visiting from Birkenhead. At the beginning of 1967, Warrington Dallam shed had an allocation of twenty-seven locomotives (seventeen 'Black 5s' plus ten 9F 2-10-0s) and it closed to steam at the beginning of October 1967. However, the depot remained open for the stabling of diesel locomotives and to provide turning and water facilities for visiting steam locomotives until August 1968 and the final end of BR main line steam. After the closure, the site remained derelict for a number of years before it was taken over for industrial use. Finally, Victorian-built ex-Midland Railway 3F No. 43189 was filmed at Warrington Bank Quay station. Alan Maund has listed this photograph as being taken during November 1959 although No. 43189 is listed as transferred to Warrington Dallam from Bescot (West Midlands) during the early summer of 1960 and withdrawn later that year. (Final Photo: *Alan Maund*)

Above and opposite page: Bickershaw Colliery (see also page 9) was to the south-east of Wigan near Leigh and the first shaft was sunk here in 1830. It was close to the Leigh branch of the Leeds & Liverpool Canal that transported coal from Bickershaw until the early 1970s. In 1973, work started to convert Bickershaw into an 'NCB Super Pit' by connecting it underground to neighbouring collieries and this had been completed by 1976. These two photographs date from April 1976 and both show Giesl ejector-equipped *Respite* that had been built by Hunslet in 1950 (W/N 3696), the standard 'Austerity' design. *Respite* worked at Bickershaw until 1978 and was later donated to the National Railway Museum.

Above and opposite page: We had planned a visit to the North-West on 4 January 1968, but due to the weather, it was postponed until 12 February. However, things were not much better on this day with fog interspersed by sleet showers as seen in these three photographs all taken at Northwich. By the beginning of 1968, there were only 359 main line steam locomotives left on BR spread between thirteen depots; the majority of these were either 'Black 5s' (151) or 8Fs (150). Northwich had an allocation of seventeen and all were Stanier 8F 2-8-0s. Prominent on the left of the first photograph are the depot's sheerlegs and used to manually lift locomotives enabling the wheels to be rolled out from underneath. Behind was the brick-built shed with four roads and to the right Northwich station can just be made out in the mix of steam and fog. Despite the row of stored and withdrawn 8Fs, there was plenty of activity here generating considerable smoke and steam effects. The depot closed to steam at the beginning of March 1968 but continued to see use well into the 1980s. The final photograph shows something else that BR would have little use for once steam had finished: a fire devil. In cold weather, this example at the west end of Northwich station by the Middlewich Road bridge was kept lit and topped up with coal (the orange glow can be seen); the resultant warmth would stop the water column to its right from freezing up. Fire devils are still used on today's heritage steam railways for the same purpose.

Above and opposite page: At the beginning of this book, we saw some photographs at Crewe works taken during a visit by the SLS (Midland Area) 'Midland Compound 1000 Special' rail tour that ran on 26 June 1960. Earlier that same day a stop for two hours was made by the tour at Ashburys, Manchester, for a visit to Gorton works plus shed, when all these photographs were taken. The Manchester, Sheffield & Lincolnshire Railway completed their Gorton workshops in 1848. Richard Peacock, who had been responsible for its planning and design, left the MS&LR in 1854 and together with Charles Beyer set up Beyer, Peacock & Company Ltd that same year; this company would become world famous in locomotive manufacture (it closed in 1966). Beyer, Peacock's Gorton foundry, was directly opposite the M&SLR's Gorton works. The first steam locomotive was constructed at Gorton works in 1858 and the last in 1951 (B1 No. 61349); the total number built here was 1,006. Sixty-four electric locomotives of Classes EM1 and EM2 were also built at Gorton works in the 1950s, the later Classes 76 and 77. In addition, overhauls of the electric locomotives were carried out here and EM1 No. 26035 is seen in pristine condition. As newly delivered, the EM1 livery was lined black but from the mid-1950s, Brunswick green was used as here. 'Royal Scot' No. 46128 *The Lovat Scouts* is on the turntable, while inside the works, locomotives under repair include Class O1 No. 63689 from Annesley shed. The last steam locomotive to have a major repair at Gorton works was No. 48520 and the very last to leave the works was electric EM2 No. 27001 on 24 May 1963; the works closed on 1 June 1963. (*Ellis James-Robertson*)

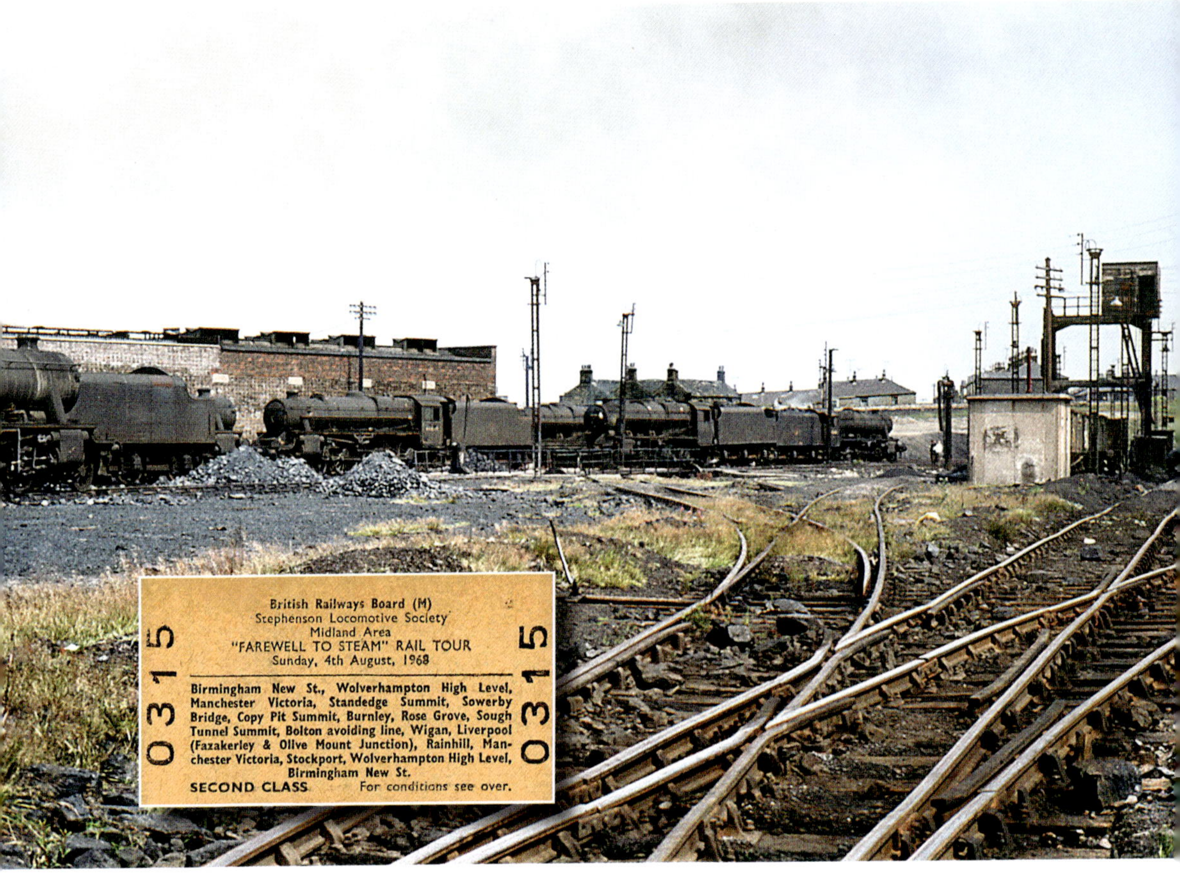
British Railways Board (M)
Stephenson Locomotive Society
Midland Area
"FAREWELL TO STEAM" RAIL TOUR
Sunday, 4th August, 1968
Birmingham New St., Wolverhampton High Level, Manchester Victoria, Standedge Summit, Sowerby Bridge, Copy Pit Summit, Burnley, Rose Grove, Sough Tunnel Summit, Bolton avoiding line, Wigan, Liverpool (Fazakerley & Olive Mount Junction), Rainhill, Manchester Victoria, Stockport, Wolverhampton High Level, Birmingham New St.
SECOND CLASS
For conditions see over.
0315
0315

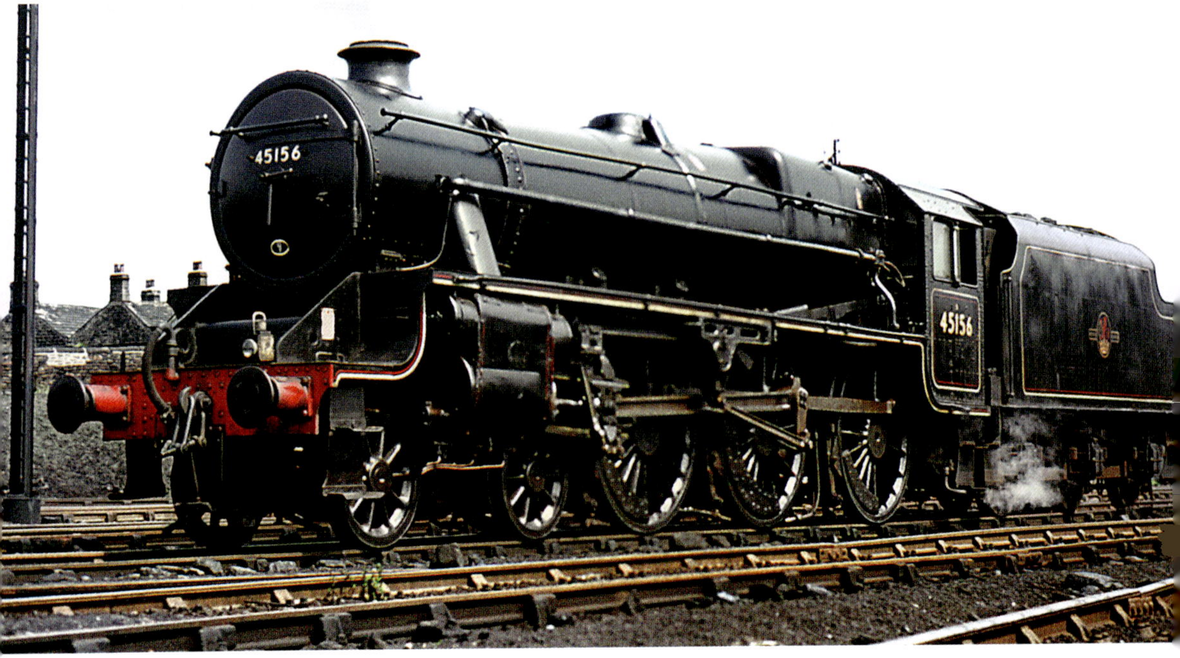
45156
45156

Above and opposite page: The delightful-sounding Rose Grove was (and still is) the first station west of Burnley on the line to Accrington and very close to the Leeds & Liverpool Canal. It was also location of one of the last three BR main line depots to remain open for steam, until the beginning of August 1968. The other two were Lostock Hall (near Preston) and Carnforth; also, BR continued to have a depot for narrow-gauge steam locomotives until 1989 (the Vale of Rheidol line at Aberystwyth). At the beginning of 1967, Rose Grove had an allocation of thirty-five locomotives, but one year later, this was down to twenty-nine (nine 'Black 5s' plus twenty 8F 2-8-0s). The author, his father, and Eric Parker only ever visited Rose Grove depot twice: Sunday 28 July 1968 (by car) and Sunday 4 August 1968 (by rail). The first two photographs are from our July visit when the depot had just one week of life remaining. There were a surprising number of steam locomotives present—thirty-six according to Eric Parker's diaries—although many were out of use and entirely made up of 'Black 5s' and 8Fs. The last surviving of the very few named 'Black 5s' was No. 45156 *Ayrshire Yeomanry* (but missing its nameplates on this day). No. 45156's tip-top external condition was because it was about to haul (with No. 45073) the joint Severn Valley Railway Society and Manchester Rail Travel Society's 'Farewell to BR Steam' rail tour. Exactly one week later, we travelled on the SLS (Midland Area) 'Farewell to Steam No. 1' rail tour (ticket included) as seen in the final photograph. We stopped at Rose Grove for forty minutes, allowing our locomotives (Nos 44871 & 44894) to take water and tour participants to enjoy a final shed visit. Today, the site of the shed building at Rose Grove is directly underneath the M65 motorway.

Above and opposite page: The first two photographs were taken by the author's school friend Michael Bailey on his Kodak Instamatic camera and show the class leaders of the 'Black 5s' and 8Fs. No. 45000 is stored out of use with sacking over its chimney at Chester shed on 16 April 1967 during the Worcester Locomotive Society's 'Thirteen Depots in Liverpool & Crewe Areas' trainspotting coach trip that we both travelled on. To fit so much into one day, these WLS trips involved very early departures from home and late arrivals back. The author had always thought No. 45000 was the first-built 'Black 5', especially as it was already listed at the time for preservation as part of the National Collection. The first-built 'Black 5' was in fact No. 45020 (built by the Vulcan Foundry and delivered in August 1934); No. 45000 was the first 'Black 5' built at the LMS's Crewe works and delivered in February 1935. The second photograph was taken at Stockport Edgeley shed on 16 July 1967 during the WLS 'Twelve Depots in Manchester area' coach tour that both of us travelled on. Of particular interest on No. 48000 is that this locomotive was one of only twelve built (out of 852) with a dome-less boiler; it had been withdrawn in March 1967. In many ways, the 8Fs were a freight version of the 'Black 5s', although it was cheaper in the 1930s to rebuild the old LNWR 0-8-0s rather than build new 8Fs. Finally, proof that No. 45000 did return to service again after its period of storage at Chester: it is at the south end of Preston station during early September 1967 acting as station pilot. No. 45000 was withdrawn from Lostock Hall shed (Preston) during October 1967 but survives in preservation at the National Railway Museum. (First two photographs: *Michael Bailey*)

Above and opposite page: The date is 20 July 1967, the time is 12.52 p.m., and the location about 1 mile south of Preston. Carlisle Kingmoor-allocated 'Britannia' No. 70011 *Hotspur* may well be working a through up parcels service from its home city to Crewe. A return working between Carlisle and Crewe at 282 miles was the highest BR daily mileage undertaken by steam at this time. Until a couple of weeks or so earlier that month, this crown was held by return workings between London Waterloo and Weymouth (285.5 miles), and up to the beginning of March 1967, the highest was a double return journey between Shrewsbury and Aberystwyth (326 miles).

The Lancashire & Yorkshire Railway's electrified route from Liverpool to Southport opened in March 1904. It was a great success with stopping trains at ten-minute intervals throughout the day from Liverpool as far as Hall Road (7½ miles), and every second service ran on to Southport. Once per hour, a non-stop train ran through in twenty-five minutes, and there were even more services at peak times. Stopping trains to Southport took thirty-seven minutes compared to fifty-four with steam. Both photographs are undated and feature BR Class 502s that were built from 1939–41. First, M28357M awaits custom at Southport Chapel Street, and secondly, M28323M heads north from Ainsdale. (*Alan Maund*)

The railway had reached Poulton-le-Sands (later renamed Morecambe) from Lancaster in 1848, and by 1850, a through route existed all the way to the West Riding of Yorkshire via the original station at Settle (now Giggleswick), Hellifield, and Skipton. The company involved was the North Western Railway, but always known as the 'Little' North Western Railway to avoid confusion with the LNWR. The Midland Railway (MR) worked this line from 1852, leased it in 1859, and finally absorbed it in 1871. A port for Irish traffic was developed at Poulton-le-Sands but proved to be less than ideal due to the tidal range; instead, the MR in conjunction with the Furness Railway used Piel, near Barrow-in-Furness. Nevertheless, the MR went on to develop their own port at nearby Heysham where deep water access was more reliable, and the railway between Morecambe and Heysham opened in 1904.

The MR was another British railway company who decided to experiment with electrification early on. By 1908, they were operating an intensive and fast (even outperforming the later London Underground) electric service that connected Heysham, Morecambe, and Lancaster. The system was 6.6 kV overhead at 25 Hz and the MR generated it themselves at Heysham. This lasted until 1951 when the original electric trains were withdrawn and replaced by steam. A BR delegation had recently visited the SNCF (French National Railways) line between Aix-les-Bains and La Roche-sur-Foron that had been converted to the industrial frequency of 50 Hz. As a result, the electrical system here in Lancashire was upgraded to 6.6 kV at 50 Hz and used as a test bed for the future 25 kV at 50 Hz of today, including use of the world's first germanium traction rectifier. It was air-cooled, rated at 750 kW, arranged for full wave rectification, and was the result of pioneering work by the British Thomson-Houston Co. Ltd. This undated photograph at Morecambe Promenade shows M28221M (Class AM1); it has a single-arm pantograph designed by the French company of Faiveley and is one of four units created in the 1950s from ex-LNWR 1914-built vehicles used in the London area. The electric service between Heysham, Morecambe, and Lancaster ceased in early 1966. (*Alan Maund*)

The boat services from Heysham mentioned in the previous commentary also went (in fact still go) to the Isle of Man, and the family summer holiday in 1964 was two weeks on the island. This was from 25 July until 8 August and when all the photographs over the next few pages were taken. We flew from Ringway (Manchester) to Ronaldsway (Isle of Man) using a Vickers Viscount of Cambrian Airways (registration number G-AMON)—the author's first ever aircraft flight. Our base was in the capital of Douglas (until Victorian times the capital was Castletown), and for one week, the author took advantage of the 'Holiday Runabout Ticket' that can be seen in the introduction on page 11. The Isle of Man Railway Company (IOMR) was registered in December 1870, and following a survey of narrow-gauge lines including the Festiniog Railway, their engineer recommended a 3-foot gauge. The first official journey, from Douglas to Peel, took place on Thursday, 1 July 1873. Finance was a problem and stringent economies led to an edict that Douglas would have 'no expensive terminal edifices', at least for a time. Yet over the fifty years or so from the mid-1870s, a continuous programme of improvements took place at Douglas station. The result was an impressive and up-to-date narrow-gauge terminal second to none. The southern island (platform faces Nos 5 and 6) in use here was generally for Port Erin line trains and the northern island platform this photograph was taken from, for Ramsey and Peel services. The time on Douglas's station clock inside the glazed circulating area says 4.38 p.m.

Looking now in the opposite direction from the west end of Douglas station and to the right of the running lines is the two-road engine shed. To the left of the shed was a single-road workshop, on the track to which the railcars are standing. On the extreme right can just be made out the remains of the coal stack, when stocks were high; this could amount to some 400 tons. The workshops were remarkably self-sufficient and also carried out work for the IOMR's own road services. It was customary to strip down only one engine at a time for heavy repairs. Boilers were supplied from Beyer, Peacock, but following closure of their locomotive manufacturing business in mid-1960s, Hunslet of Leeds was used. In 1961, the IOMR purchased two County Donegal Railways Joint Committee railcars; the system had closed to all traffic on 1 January 1960. They were CDRJC Nos 19 (entered service in January 1950) and 20 (entered service in January 1951) and were the last power units built for the company. Motive power came from a Gardner 6LW engine; the power bogie plus cab unit were supplied by Walker Brothers of Wigan, but the carriage portion was built at the ex-Great Northern Railway of Ireland works at Dundalk; and the carriage portion was articulated to the engine unit. The IOMR paid £160 for each railcar, £165 for dismantling and carriage to Londonderry, and £250 for shipping to the island; No. 19 had cost over £8,000 when new. They were landed at Douglas in May 1961 and on the IOMR were coupled back to back. By 1963, the railcars alone provided a quarter of passenger train mileage and ran both the Peel and Port Erin lines in the winter. At the time of our visit, the railcars were used on a service from Douglas to Kirkmichael for the Glen Wyllin pleasure grounds (owned by the IOMR).

The 15⅜-mile-long line from Douglas to here at Port Erin is the only survivor of the IOMR and is today run as a heritage/tourist railway, making it the longest narrow-gauge steam line in Britain still using its original locomotives and coaches. 1905-built 2-4-0T No. 11 *Maitland* (named after an official of the IOMR) awaits custom before returning to Douglas in the summer of 1964. This locomotive had a new boiler fitted in 1959, the very last supplied by Beyer, Peacock. The platform at Port Erin is in two parts and continues behind the photographer. Between the two platform sections was this public crossing; its right-of-way forbade the railway to block it with stationary trains.

Cutting across the middle of the island was the first line to open, from Douglas to Peel (11½ miles). Peel station was built on waste ground between the harbour and gas works, and the station buildings dated from a major rebuilding in the early twentieth century. The engine shed plus water tank were by a level crossing of Mill Road, and the red building behind still exists today (a traditional Manx kipper curing house). Of the sixteen IOMR locomotives, fifteen were 2-4-0Ts, and all from Beyer, Peacock. The first built dated from 1873 and the last, 1926; this is No. 5 *Mona* (the Manx name for the island) from 1874.

Above and opposite page: The Manx Northern Railway (MNR) came about because the IOMR had no intention of extending its network to the north of the island. The MNR was formed in 1877, the first sod was cut in March 1878, and it opened in August 1879 from St John's (on the Douglas to Peel line) to Ramsey and its quay. The bill for a third railway company, the Foxdale Railway (FR), was introduced in May 1883 to connect with a lead mining area in the hills about 2½ miles south of St John's, but before construction of the FR had started, it was leased to the MNR. It has been said the MNR thought they had got their hands on a commercial lead mine that was a financial gold mine, but it proved to be a noose. As with all the Isle of Man photographs, these three date from the summer of 1964 and the first shows the derelict terminus at Foxdale. The branch from St John's was at a continuous grade of 1 in 48.6, and at Foxdale, one of the sidings climbed at 1 in 12. To cope with this, the locomotive in the second photograph was built in 1885 by Dübs & Co., Glasgow. This was MNR No. 4 (later IOMR No. 15) *Caledonia*, an 0-6-0T with 27 tons adhesive weight and around double the tractive effort of any other engine on the island at the time (according to author J. I. C. Boyd); it is seen inside the Douglas shed and workshop complex. However, tonnages dwindled; the FR went into voluntary liquidation during 1891, and the last lead mine closed in 1911. From then only spoil trains plus infrequent passenger and general goods services used the branch. The final Foxdale branch workings were to remove track for use elsewhere on 22 and 26 January 1960. The MNR suffered the expense of the FR plus fierce competition (after the late 1890s) from the electric tramway between Douglas and Ramsey. This resulted in an act of 1904 that permitted the IOMR to absorb the MNR and FR. The final photograph shows a Ramsey to Douglas service passing over Glen Mooar viaduct; this consisted of three 60-foot lattice steel spans on stone piers 75 feet high. The viaduct was along a 3-mile coastal strip that included the summit of the line between St John's and Ramsey. There were concerns over this viaduct; additional bracing was added in 1914 together with weight limits plus a speed restriction, and it was rebuilt with new spans in 1921.

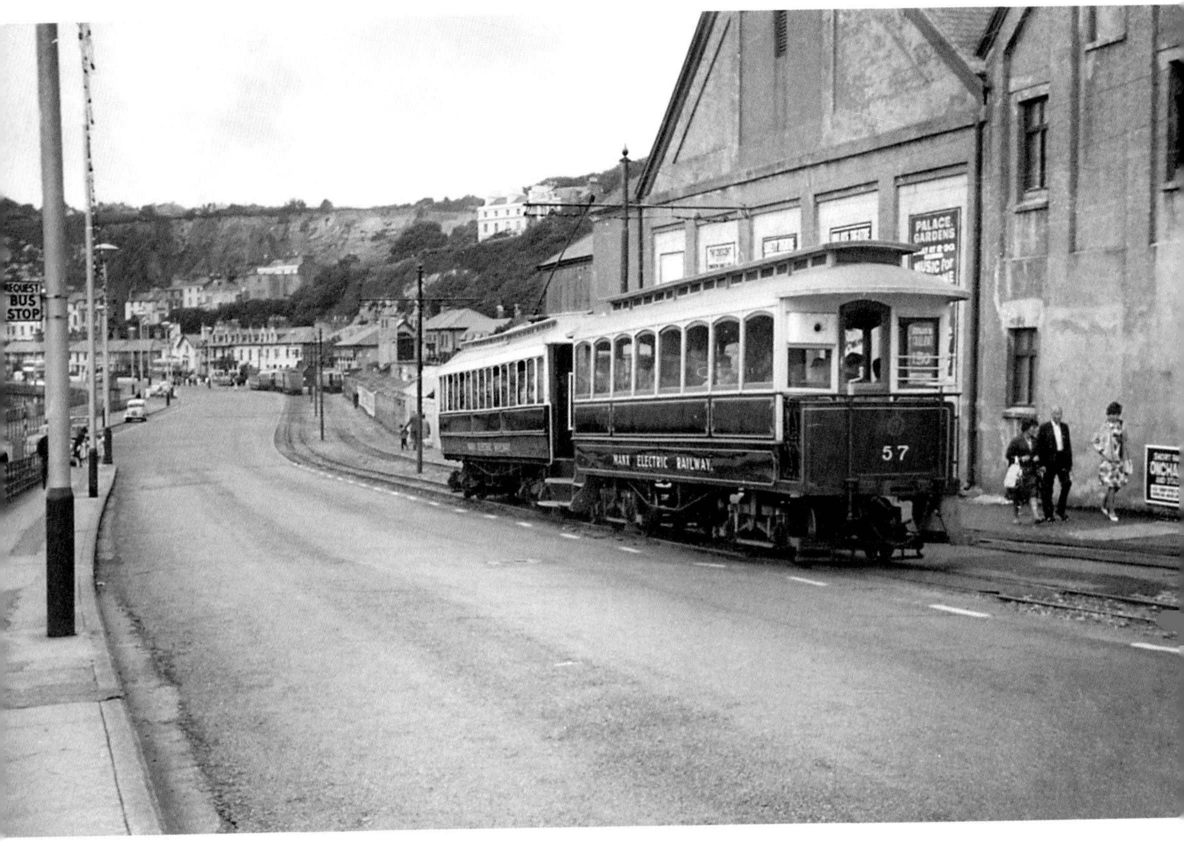
REQUEST
BUS
STOP
PALACE
GARDENS
MANX ELECTRIC RAILWAY
57

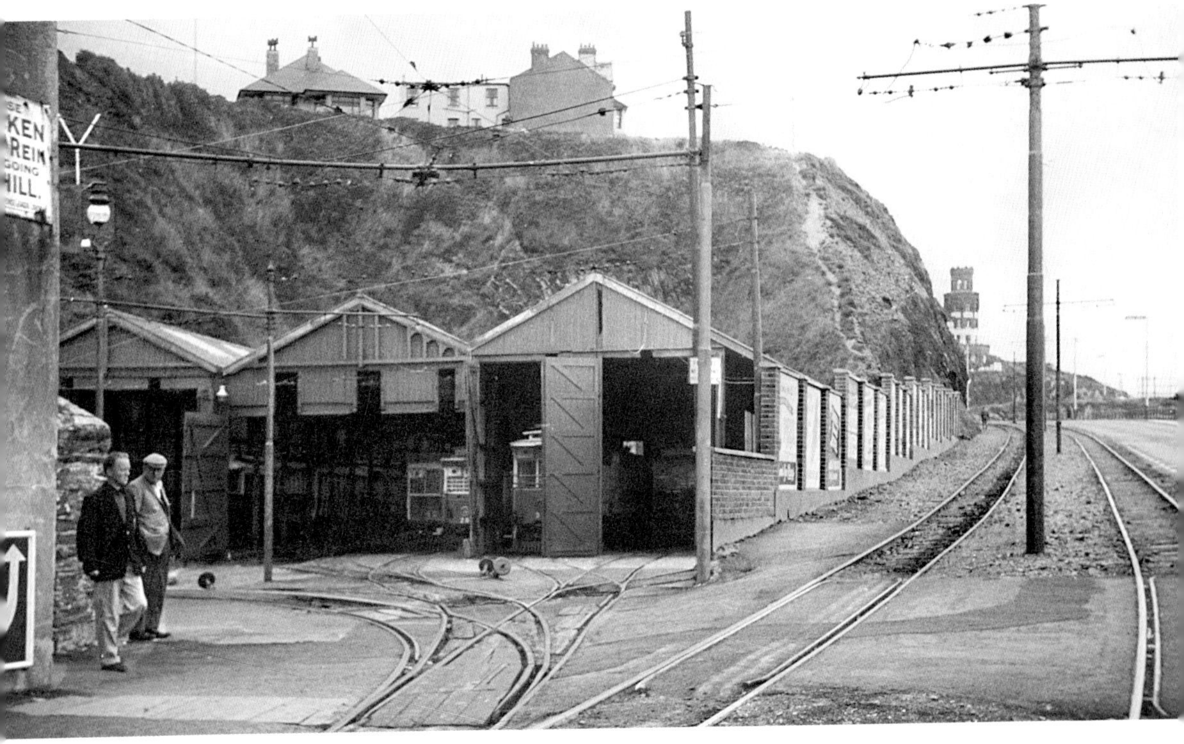

Above and opposite page: The Manx Electric Railway was unique within the British Isles—a narrow-gauge electrically worked light railway (but not constructed under the later Light Railways Act). The MER formerly carried a fair quantity of freight traffic but of recent decades relies mainly on tourists. The first section from Douglas to Groudle Glen was authorised in 1892 and opened the year after; an extension to Laxey then followed in July 1894, and the final part to Ramsey opened throughout in August 1899. This rapid expansion strained finances and the line went in to receivership; the assets were then purchased by a syndicate of Manchester businessmen and the MER was formed in 1902. Profitability raised its head again in the mid-1950s resulting in Nationalization by the Manx government. The MER is built to a gauge of 3 feet, is 17 miles long (double throughout at the time of our visit), and has electricity supplied by overhead wire at 550 V DC. It is the oldest electric tram line in the world whose original rolling stock is still in service. All the photographs date from the summer of 1964 and the first two are at Douglas close to the Derby Castle depot looking in opposite directions.

The Snaefell Mountain Railway in the final photograph was built as the Snaefell Mountain Tramway in 1895 from near the MER at Laxey to the summit of the island's highest mountain: Snaefell (2,034 feet); it was taken over by the MER in 1902. The ruling gradient is 1 in 12, very steep for a line worked by adhesion only; it does have a centre rail using the Fell system that is solely for braking purposes. The gauge is 3 feet 6 inches (6 inches greater than the MER and IOMR) and the overhead power is at 550 V DC. During construction, an extra rail was used to allow the great tractive power of *Caledonia* (see previous commentary) to be employed on this line's fearsome grades; it was shipped from Ramsey to Laxey and then taken through the town on baulks and rollers. The 1895-built Car No. 3 (destroyed in a runaway during March 2016) is seen at the summit of Snaefell with its bow collector system prominent; once common across Europe, this method of electricity collection was generally replaced in later years by pantographs or trolley poles.

Above and opposite page: Two photographs taken at Oxenholme during July 1963: first, No. 42210 stands by the 1943-constructed Oxenholme No. 2 signal box at the south end of the station; this was demolished in 1973. At the north end, No. 48775 passes with a partially fitted express freight. Built in 1937, it was requisitioned by the War Department (WD) and only came back to BR service in 1957. No. 48775 was then withdrawn in the mass cull of Scottish Region steam at the end of 1962 only to be reinstated a short time later. Final withdrawal came in August 1968 from Lostock Hall; of note is this locomotive's oversize WD top feed. (*Alan Maund*)

Above, below, and opposite page: Now a move to the Cumbrian Coast with a series of photographs taken during July 1973; these begin with a panoramic view of Whitehaven harbour. The former Quaker Oats factory is prominent and coal wagons are dotted about; coal traffic ceased here following the end of mining at nearby Haig Colliery in the 1980s. One of the locomotives that worked at Haig Colliery is seen in the second photograph trundling along some very rickety-looking track south of the pit. This is 0-4-0T *King* that been constructed by Andrew Barclay of Kilmarnock in 1919 (W/N 1448). It had moved to the area from Bank Hall Colliery, Burnley, and where it had been fitted with a Giesl ejector chimney.

Finally, a view from the top of the spectacular Corkickle Brake, but also known by other names such as Marchon Brake or just 'The Brake'. This cable-worked incline (reputedly the last of its kind in the country) was constructed in 1881 to handle coal from Croft pit, but following the Great Depression, it was abandoned. However, by the mid-1950s, Marchon Products had become established in the area, a major producer of detergent chemicals. This traffic plus that from nearby collieries all went down the Howgill Brake to Whitehaven harbour, but it was too much and thoughts turned to reactivating the long-disused Corkickle Brake. It was handed over by the NCB, modernised, and became fully operational in May 1955. Business looks to be thriving on this July 1973 day in a view taken from the control cabin atop the winding house. The steepest grade involved was 1 in 5.2; there are three rails on the top section, four at the passing loop, with two rails (single track) from the loop. The railway visible in the distance at the top of the photograph stretching from left to right is that from Whitehaven to Carnforth; the incline closed in 1986.

Above and opposite page: And now, two photographs from June 1972 taken during a visit to industrial railway sites across Cumbria. Both are at Solway Colliery, Workington, and feature 0-4-0ST *Solway No. 2* built by Hudswell Clarke in 1948 (W/N 1814), but basking in seeming anonymity at this time. Solway was Workington's last deep coal mine and it closed in 1973. The author very much appreciates the help given with the last five photographs by John Harkness (an ex-engine driver at Harrington colliery, Lowca) plus Peter Burgess and his website (www.cumbria-railways.co.uk).

On the author's car journeys with his father to Scotland from Worcestershire in the late 1950s and early 1960s, a stop would be made at an overbridge just north of Shap summit. Here, the car would be topped up using jerrycans brought with us, but it also gave the opportunity to see comings and goings on the WCML. These photographs were taken on our northbound journey during Easter 1963. Newton Heath, Manchester-allocated 'Rebuilt Patriot' No. 45522 *Prestatyn* heads south climbing towards Shap summit in the first photograph. No. 43035 in the second was based at Tebay and is heading north with the family Vauxhall Cresta on the bridge.

In the mid-nineteenth century, iron works in Cumbria needed coal and coke that was available in County Durham, while the iron works on Teesside and at Consett needed rich haematite ore from Cumbria to mix with low-grade local Cleveland ore. There were schemes in the 1840s for a railway across the Pennines and much was made of this heavy mineral traffic in both directions by promoters, but not passenger potential through this sparsely populated area. The South Durham & Lancashire Union Railway (SD&LUR) was granted royal assent in July 1857 to build a line from Bishop Auckland, via Barnard Castle, then over the Pennines to Kirkby Stephen, and on to Tebay (on the WCML of today). In spite of the difficult terrain, the 35-mile section from Barnard Castle via Stainmore summit (1,370 feet) to Tebay was open for mineral traffic in July 1861, with formal opening taking place a month later. In the interests of economy, engineer Thomas Bouch (designer of the ill-fated original Tay Bridge) preferred to work round the contours instead of tunnelling, but at the expense of distance and steepness, especially on the western ascent. Bouch did, however, resort to viaducts in some quantity, and used up much of the originally authorised company capital in the process.

On Thursday, 17 August 1961, Ellis James-Robertson made a journey across the Pennines over the Stainmore route from here at Barnard Castle to Penrith. Although an earlier station already existed at Barnard Castle (later used as the town's goods depot), it was not suitably placed for extending the railway westwards. The station in the photograph was built instead and opened in August 1861 and had received this new canopy after the Second World War. Passenger services finally ceased through Barnard Castle (the Middleton-in-Teesdale branch) in November 1964 and freight in April 1965. (*Ellis James-Robertson*)

Barras is the third station to the west of Barnard Castle on the old SD&LUR over the Pennines, often referred to as the Stainmore route. Most stations had opened with the line in August 1861, but Barras only opened for freight at this time and first appeared in a public timetable during February 1862; it is a remote and thinly populated location. At the time, Barras was the highest main line station in England (1,100 feet), losing this claim to fame in 1887 when Dent (1,150 feet) opened on the Settle to Carlisle route. Freight facilities were withdrawn here on and from 1 December 1952, also, Barras was reduced to the status of an unstaffed halt at the same time. DMUs were introduced in January 1958 operating out of Darlington diesel depot and cut about twenty-five minutes from the steam schedule, but no additional services were put on. In the spring of 1961, there were three return journeys over the entire 63¾ miles from Darlington to Penrith plus an extra return working on Saturdays only from Penrith to Appleby East (but nothing on Sundays). Ellis James-Robertson travelled on 17 August 1961 from Barnard Castle to Penrith on the mid-morning service and there is a note in his records saying 'Barras E50644', perhaps the number of the lead unit. (*Ellis James-Robertson*)

Between Barnard Castle and Kirkby Stephen, the railway was steeply graded (maximum 1 in 59), relatively lightly laid (LNER RA 5 in the 1930s), and notable for its graceful viaducts. When opened, this section was single track with sufficient land for double, and all but three of the viaducts were built for double track; eventually everything was doubled. The first photograph is another from 17 August 1961 and shows the most famous of the viaducts—Belah, looking to the west (1,040 feet long and 196 feet high). Secondly, taken on 4 September 1955, is Deepdale viaduct looking to the east (740 feet long and 161 feet high). (Colour photo: *Ellis James-Robertson*)

The joint Stephenson Locomotive Society (SLS) and Manchester Locomotive Society (MLS) 'Northern Dales' rail tour ran on Sunday, 4 September 1955 (ticket included). It is first seen at Tebay where there was a locomotive change from Blackpool-allocated 'Compound' No. 41102 to J21 No. 65061 coupled with Ivatt Class 2 No. 46478 (both Darlington-allocated) for a run over the Stainmore route. In the second photograph, the pair is seen at Kirkby Stephen East where there was a twenty-five-minute stop. The previous page also includes a photograph taken during the course of this rail tour.

In early 1959, rumours started to circulate about the closure of the Stainmore route. The freight traffic was diverted away via Carlisle and Newcastle in July 1960. The minister gave his approval for withdrawal of the passenger service in December 1961, and the last trains ran on 20 January 1962. These two views show derelict stations in March 1967: first, a rather eerie-looking Bowes. No restoration work has taken place here; instead, the station buildings have just decayed and collapsed over the decades. Secondly, at Kirkby Stephen East, the track just visible served Merrygill (Hartley) Quarry until the mid-1970s; this station is nowadays a railway heritage centre.

Penrith station is seen on 17 August 1961 at the end of a journey over the Stainmore route that we have followed over the last few pages. The 'For Ullswater' on the station sign dated from early BR days and it reverted back to just Penrith in 1974; today, it is called Penrith North Lakes. The Eden Valley Railway (EVR) constructed the line from Kirkby Stephen via Appleby to Penrith that this DMU has just travelled over. It joined the Lancaster & Carlisle Railway (today's WCML) at Clifton, 4 miles south of Penrith. The first sod of the EVR was cut in August 1858 at Appleby; it opened for mineral traffic in April 1862, and passenger services started in the June but it took over one year before a convenient connection was made with the L&CR at what became Eden Valley Junction. The EVR was built as single track with sufficient land for double. The SD&LUR plus the EVR were worked by the Stockton & Darlington Railway from the outset, and that company took them over in June 1862 only to then be taken over themselves by the North Eastern Railway (NER) in 1863. The return service back to Darlington from Penrith stands to the left and Ellis has written in his notes 'E50622', perhaps the lead car number of the DMU. The old EVR closed to passengers at the same time as the SD&LUR and the last trains ran on 20 January 1962 (some specific freight traffic was retained). To the right, 'Princess' pacific No. 46211 *Queen Maud* has charge of the 10.05 a.m. Glasgow to Birmingham through train. (*Ellis James-Robertson*)

Ellis James-Robertson has now arrived at Carlisle on 17 August 1961, and this view is looking south from the north end of the station. When the West Coast Route was planned, negotiations opened in October 1846 for the building of a joint station here on land purchased by the L&CR. Carlisle Citadel station opened in 1847 and connecting lines were laid in, but construction costs and maintenance were considerable and its allocation to users became contentious. A (Carlisle) Citadel Station Joint Committee was set up in 1857 and formalised by an Act of Parliament in 1861. The gradual admission of other companies caused the station to be entirely rebuilt so that it eventually covered some ten acres with eight platforms; the platform area alone was over 2 acres. By the Grouping, seven companies were at Citadel station: the London & North Western, Caledonian, Glasgow & South Western, Midland, Maryport & Carlisle, North British, and North Eastern railways. It was said Carlisle station was busier at midnight than it was at midday. Freight traffic did not pass through Citadel and instead used its own tracks controlled by another committee to the west of the station (closed in the 1980s).

This photograph was taken with FP3 film at settings of 250/5.6 plus a yellow filter, and the time is about 1.45 p.m. On the left is No. 46240 *City of Coventry*, the station pilot in the middle is 'Jinty' No. 47358, and to the right is No. 46226 *Duchess of Norfolk*. (*Ellis James-Robertson*)

Above and opposite page: The SLS (Midland Area) 'Pacific Pennine Three Summits' tour ran on 12 July 1964 and stopped directly outside Carlisle Kingmoor engine shed for the benefit of participants, over ninety locomotives were present. No. 46251 *City of Nottingham* hauled the train from Birmingham, and from Carlisle to Leeds No. 46255 *City of Hereford* was used (it had been hoped to provide eponymous No. 46238 *City of Carlisle*); note the different liveries. The June 1964 SLS house magazine hinted this tour could be a 'farewell' for the 'Coronation' pacifics, and so it proved as all were withdrawn by the end of September. The author's ticket is included.

The terminus at Alston features in the first photograph taken during March 1970. Under the 'Beeching Axe', the line from Haltwhistle was slated for closure, but because of the poor road network, it survived for a time. By 1969, Alston was an unstaffed halt and eventually it closed at the beginning of May 1976. Next are the works underway on 17 August 1961 leading to the abandonment of Farnley Scar Tunnel (170 yards), east of Corbridge on the line from Carlisle to Newcastle. Originally single track, the tunnel was doubled in 1844, but abandoned and bypassed to the south, opening in May 1962. (Second photograph: *Ellis James-Robertson*)

On 30 August 1959, our friend Alan Maund travelled on an SLS tour hauled by Midland Railway 'Compound' No. 1000 that included a visit to Doncaster where these photographs were taken. In a row of what appears to be newly constructed diesels, the only number resolvable is that of the second—Loughborough-built D5546. No. 60090 *Grand Parade* had a 'Heavy Intermediate' repair here that summer and looks spotless. This locomotive received its double chimney the year previously, would gain trough-type smoke deflectors in early 1963, but would be withdrawn in October 1963 from St Rollox (Balornock) shed, Glasgow. (*Alan Maund*)

First, another photograph taken at Doncaster on 30 August 1959. What later became the Class 03 lightweight diesel shunters were being built here and although a number cannot be seen, the *Railway Observer* reported that on 15 August 1959, D2066–69 were under construction. Alan also visited Doncaster on 11 October 1964 during a Warwickshire Railway Society tour hauled by 'Merchant Navy' No. 35007 *Aberdeen Commonwealth* (see also page 82). By this time, Doncaster works had ceased repairing steam but the works' service locomotives were present. This is Departmental Locomotive No. 11, a J50 0-6-0T previously No. 68914 when in capital stock. (*Alan Maund*)

Almost anything using coal and steam would be recorded (a steam lorry appears on page 128) and this lovely photograph is of PS *Lincoln Castle*. Built on the Clyde in the early years of the Second World War, this triple expansion paddle steamer (PS) was used by the LNER for their ferry service across the Humber between New Holland and Hull. Additions included radar plus an enclosed wheel house in 1948. PS *Lincoln Castle* continued on the same duties until withdrawn in May 1978 due to the condition of its boiler, and it remained coal-fired until the end. A new life then beckoned as a pub at Hessle close to the Humber Bridge. In 1987, PS *Lincoln Castle* was resold and moved to Immingham for refurbishment but by 2010, the ship was scrapped. This photograph dates from June 1974 and was taken at New Holland Pier.

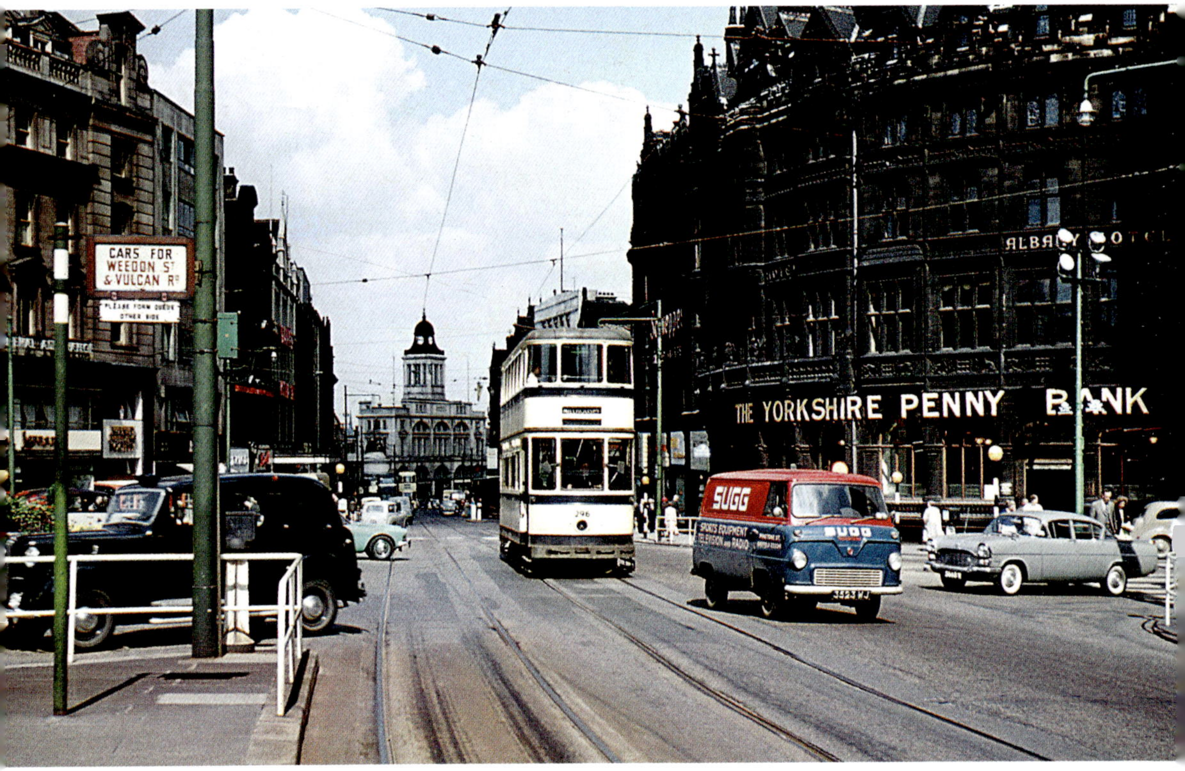
CARS FOR
WEEDON ST
& VULCAN RD
PLEASE FORM QUEUE
OTHER SIDE
THE YORKSHIRE PENNY BANK
SUGG

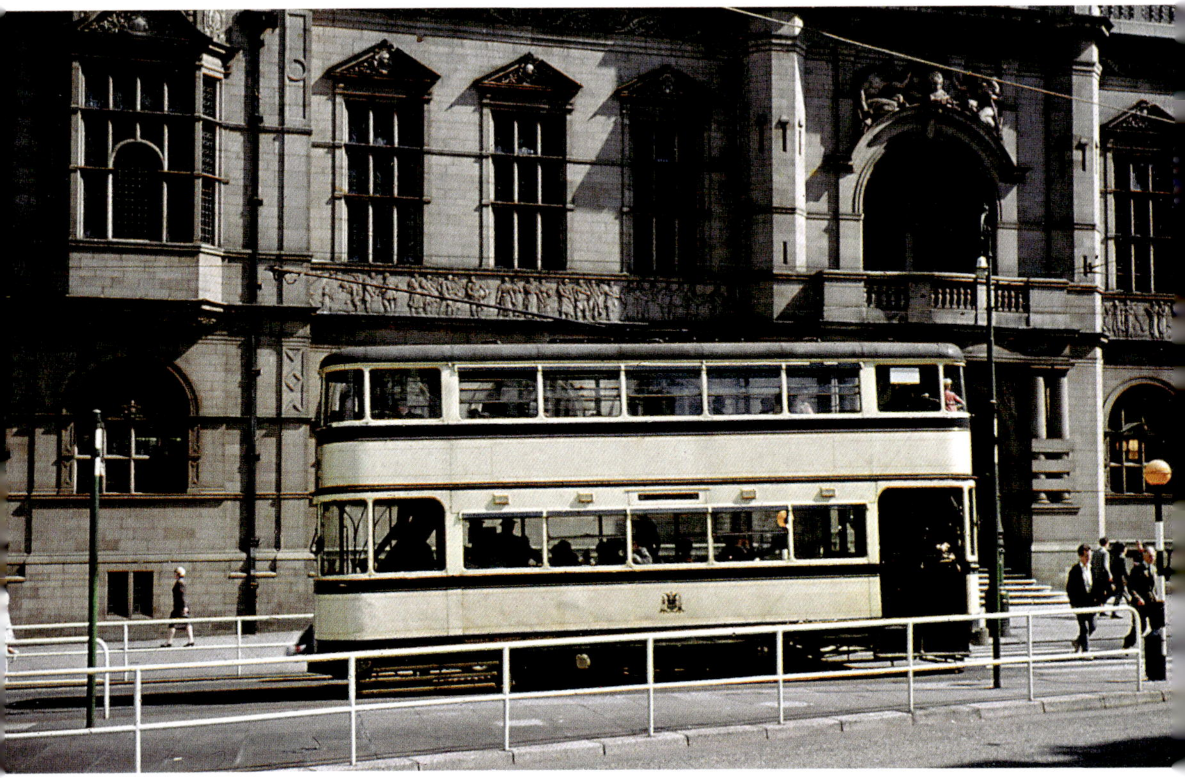

Above and opposite page: Ellis James-Robertson visited Sheffield to photograph its tram system on 10 August 1960 in the course of a journey from North Wales to the Northallerton area. The first tram line in the city was horse-drawn and opened in 1873. Sheffield Corporation took over the network in 1896 and very soon recommended electrification on the overhead system using power locally generated; at its greatest extent, 100 miles of tram routes were operated. The last extensions to the network were opened during 1934, but in 1951, the decision was taken to eventually close the system and replace it with motor buses. The final route to remain open was from Beauchief to Vulcan Road, and this closed on Saturday, 8 October 1960—the last city tramway in England. But the trams are back and in 1994, the 'Sheffield Supertram' system opened.

The first photograph is looking along Fargate. The Yorkshire Penny Bank became the Yorkshire Bank Ltd in 1959 (its centenary year) and until recently has occupied the same building. Locally built car No. 296 dated from just before the Second World War and had a seating capacity of sixty-one. The building in the background of the second photograph is Sheffield Town Hall. Finally, we see Vulcan Road, terminus of the route from Beauchief; this location is close to the Meadowhall Shopping Centre of today. Car No. 522 is one of thirty-five built from 1950–52 by Charles Roberts & Co. of Wakefield with a seating capacity of sixty-two; these were the ultimate in UK-designed and built four-wheel tramcars. See also page 13. (*Ellis James-Robertson*)

The author and his father travelled on the joint SLS/MLS 'Whitby Moors' rail tour that ran on Saturday, 6 March 1965 (see also page 84). The tour had started from Manchester Victoria with 'Jubilee' No. 45698 *Mars* and here at Wakefield Kirkgate it was replaced by a locomotive already in private ownership, No. 3442 *The Great Marquess*. No. 45698 has a prominent yellow cab-side stripe and this indicated it was not allowed to work over the 25-kV electrified lines south of Crewe from the beginning of September 1964. With tour participants thronging on the platform, WD 2-8-0 No. 90516 passed through with a coal train.

This is South Kirkby colliery, Yorkshire, during a November 1970 visit. These locomotives are the standard Hunslet 16-inch-diameter cylinder 0-6-0ST built from 1923 to 1958: *John Shaw* (W/N 2375/1942) and *Kinsley* (W/N1954/1939). Coal from South Kirkby was one of the types used for locomotive testing by BR. It had a calorific value of 13,850 British Thermal Units (BTUs) as received (14,140 dry) and was described as Grade 1A, South Yorkshire Hard (dull, large, no dust); its characteristics made it much favoured for locomotive firing, the highest continuous powers ever achieved on test used this coal. With No. 71000 *Duke of Gloucester*, it cost £3 16s 6d per ton loaded on the tender.

Above and opposite page: All three photographs date from the beginning of October 1970 and show Hudswell Clarke-built 0-6-0T steam locomotives that were modified to try and improve their performance. The first two are from a visit to Peckfield colliery, Micklefield, Yorkshire. The first ceremonial sod here was cut in 1874; it opened in 1877 but suffered a terrible disaster in 1896 when sixty-three men and boys were killed. This locomotive is Hudswell Clarke W/N 1822 that was delivered new from their Leeds works in April 1949 to Whitwood colliery. The 'S.100.' on its side indicates 'Steam' and the serial number '100' in the North Yorkshire Area numbering system; this locomotive arrived at Peckfield in the early 1960s. Between June 1964 and July 1965, it was overhauled and modified at the Hunslet works in Leeds; this including a new steel firebox, mechanical stoker, and a new blastpipe arrangement. A diesel arrival in the summer of 1972 marked the end of steam at Peckfield, but S.100. was not scrapped and instead survives on the Chacewater Railway; Peckfield colliery closed in 1980.

The final photograph is of another Hudswell Clarke 0-6-0T, W/N 1844 of 1951, and this time the location is Water Haigh colliery, Woodlesford, Yorkshire. This was a relatively new colliery as its two main shafts were sunk in 1910; it was also very close to the Aire & Calder Navigation for shipment of coal in addition to road and rail transport. Whit No. 4 stands for Whitwood No. 4 (this locomotive was at Whitwood colliery throughout much of the 1950s), and the modifications it received included a Kylpor exhaust ejector, underfeed stoker, plus an on-grate type of secondary air provision. Water Haigh colliery closed in 1970 but Whit No. 4 continued here with clearance of coal ground stock, eventually moving to Prince of Wales colliery, Pontefract, in 1971; it did not survive to be preserved.

A1 No. 60120 *Kittiwake* departs Leeds City with the London, King's Cross-bound 'Harrogate Sunday Pullman' in late afternoon sunshine on 8 October 1961 (services to King's Cross would normally have used Leeds Central station). Leeds City station came about in May 1938 when two previous stations here (Wellington and New) were combined and No. 60120 is leaving from the one-time MR Leeds Wellington station; the signal box is Leeds City Wellington (see also page 14). Further to the left is the clock tower of Leeds Town Hall showing a time of around 4.20 p.m. On the extreme right, previous to 1938 was Leeds New; this had opened in 1869 and was joint station with the London & North Western and North Eastern railways. The shed plate reads 56C—Copley Hill, Leeds—and very well presented No. 60120 had only returned from Doncaster works just over one month previously where it had received a 'general' repair including change of boiler. This would be the locomotive's last works visit and it was withdrawn at the beginning of 1964. (*Ellis James-Robertson*)

We have seen this special train previously on page 66, the SLS (Midland Area) 'Pacific Pennine Three Summits' tour that ran on 12 July 1964, and this time my father's ticket is included. Health and safety regimes were years into the future as enthusiasts throng over the platforms and tracks at Leeds City station. This station was in the throes of a further re-modelling and this time would enable closure of Leeds Central station (in 1967). All the city's passenger services would then be concentrated on the rebuilt City station including those to London, King's Cross. A century previously, Leeds was served by six railway companies working into five main stations.

The tour arrived here from Carlisle behind No. 46255 *City of Hereford* that has now been replaced by 'Jubilee' No. 45647 *Sturdee* for the run to Crewe. Our eleven coaches weighed some 400 tons, and this was above the limit allowed for a 'Jubilee' over the third summit (Standedge) mentioned in the tour name. The early days of the 'Jubilees' in the mid-1930s were fraught with problems and they were much maligned for their performance, the problem appeared to be a lack of steaming ability and the LMS commenced a lengthy series of investigations into their problems; even towards the end of the 1950s, BR was still investigating the class at the Rugby Locomotive Testing Station. Nevertheless, an excellent climb was made by No. 45647 and one of the author's friends said he had never heard a 'Jubilee' work so hard in his life. A tape recording was made of this climb and it can be listened to in the Sound Bites section of the author's website: michaelclemensrailways.co.uk.

The SLS (Midland Area) 'LMS Compound Special to Doncaster & York' rail tour (ticket included) ran on 17 June 1956. It was hauled throughout by Saltley, Birmingham-allocated No. 40928 that is seen preparing for its return from York. An interesting locomotive inside the shed here was Departmental Locomotive No. 55. Five of these diminutive 0-4-0Ts were built by the North Eastern Railway (NER) for use at Hull docks in 1890; they became LNER Class Y8. No. 55 was transferred from capital stock in June 1954 and proved most useful as shed pilot because with all but the very largest, it was possible to get this and another locomotive on the turntable together.

No. 60121 *Silurian* is seen running through light engine during August 1963 in the first of two photographs at York taken from almost the same position on the station platform. The second dates from mid-afternoon on 13 August 1960 and J72 0-6-0T No. 68736 is the station pilot. It had been repainted at Darlington works during April 1960 in NER fully-lined green livery together with BR and NER crests. Stanier 8F 2-8-0 No. 48654 of Rowsley shed awaits the road with a southbound freight and to its right on the platform is 'The Scarborough Flyer' headboard. (Second photo: *Ellis James-Robertson*)

Above and opposite page: The 'Merchant Navy' class worked in the south of England but on 11 October 1964, No. 35007 *Aberdeen Commonwealth* visited York with the Warwickshire Railway Society's 'York & Doncaster' tour. Something else that aroused enthusiasts' interest was the use of 9F 2-10-0s on passenger services; conventional wisdom dictated their plethora of 5-foot diameter wheels would preclude use at passenger train speeds. Yet, in another photograph taken by Ellis James-Robertson on 13 August 1960, Wellingborough-allocated No. 92052 arrives at York with a Yarmouth to Newcastle working at 4.07 p.m., just after the exploits of 9F classmate *Evening Star* on express services between Cardiff and London. (First photo: *Alan Maund*, second photo: *Ellis James-Robertson*)

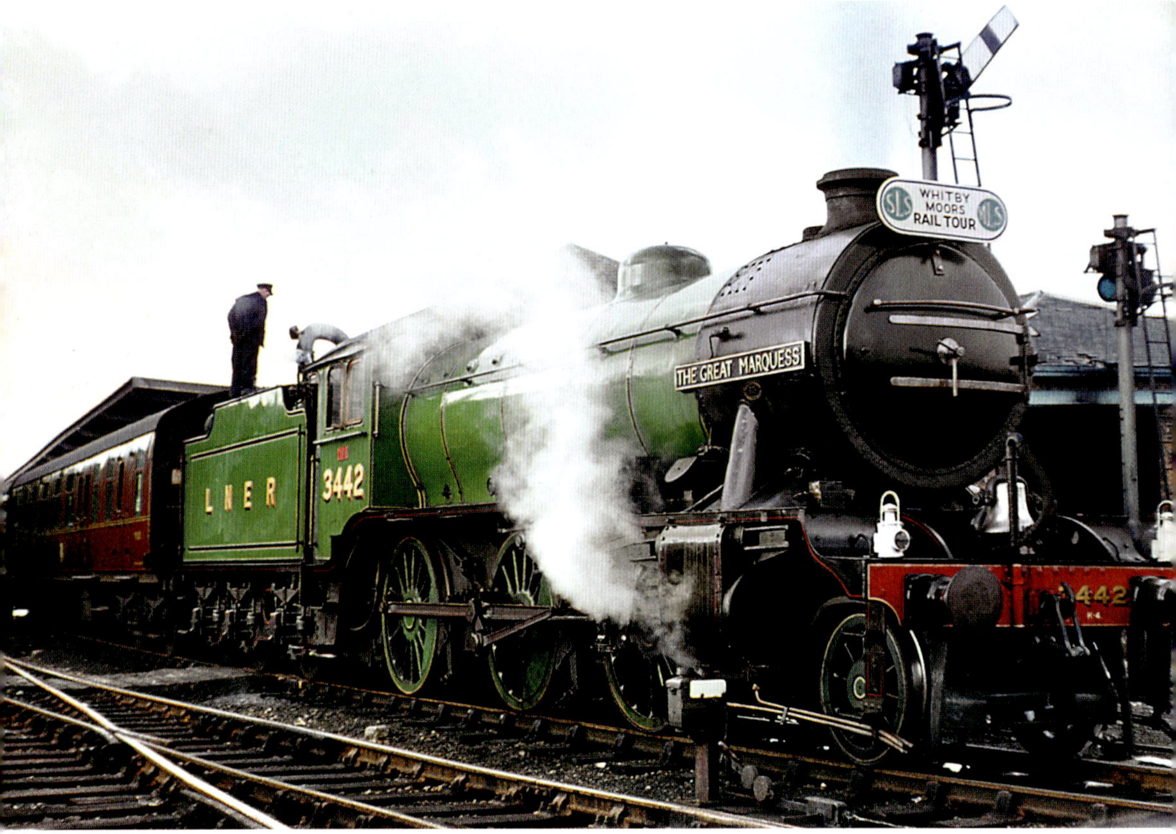

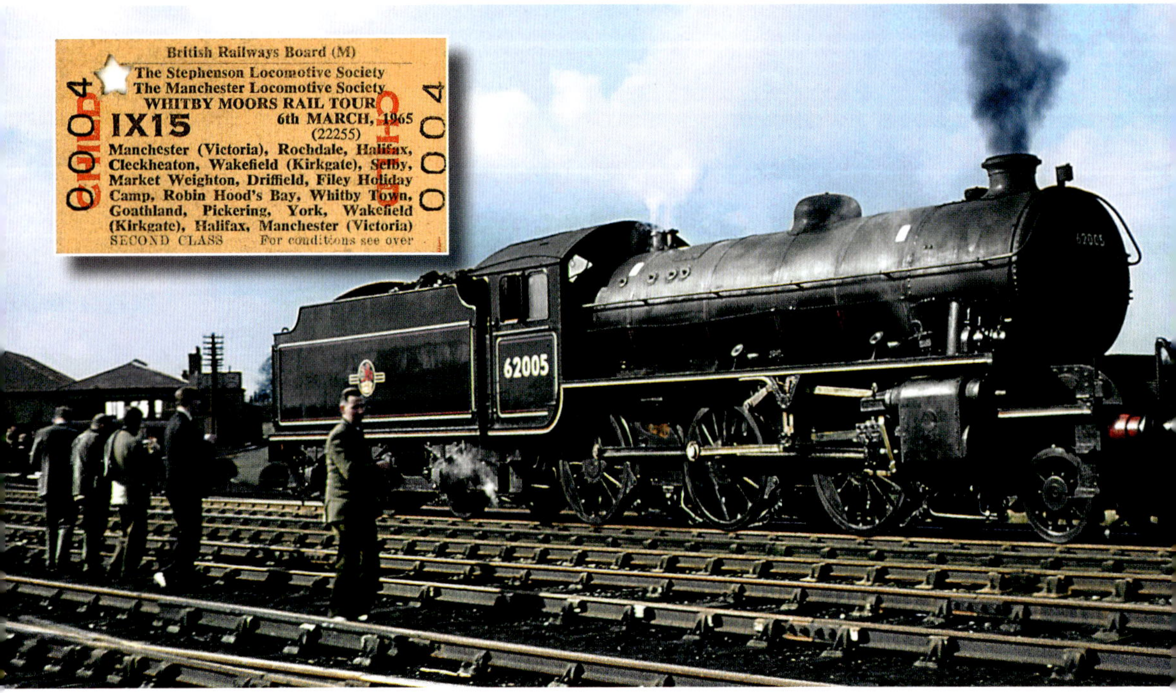

0004
British Railways Board (M)
The Stephenson Locomotive Society
The Manchester Locomotive Society
WHITBY MOORS RAIL TOUR
IX15 6th MARCH, 1965
(22255)
Manchester (Victoria), Rochdale, Halifax, Cleckheaton, Wakefield (Kirkgate), Selby, Market Weighton, Driffield, Filey Holiday Camp, Robin Hood's Bay, Whitby Town, Goathland, Pickering, York, Wakefield (Kirkgate), Halifax, Manchester (Victoria)
SECOND CLASS For conditions see over
CHILD
0004

Above and opposite page: This rail tour has been seen before on page 74 at Wakefield Kirkgate, the joint SLS/MLS 'Whitby Moors' rail tour that ran on Saturday, 6 March 1965 (the author's ticket included). From Wakefield Kirkgate, it was hauled by preserved K4 2-6-0 No. 3442 *The Great Marquess*; Viscount Garnock had acquired this locomotive in 1963 and it is in a livery of LNER apple green. The three-cylinder K4s were designed by Gresley to cope with increasing passenger traffic in West Scotland. Over the West Highland line, the earlier K2 class had a load limit of 220 tons; with the K4s, this was increased to 300 tons. The first two photographs are taken at Market Weighton where extra power was attached in the form of two-cylinder K1 2-6-0 No. 62005 in the second photograph. This locomotive was not long out of Darlington works where it had received a 'general' repair and is in BR-lined black livery. This locomotive was also preserved and initial thoughts were that as K1s and K4s shared the same type of boiler; No. 62005 would be the source of a spare for No. 3442. This was not needed; instead No. 62005 was restored and has been a regular performer itself on the West Highland line in recent summers. The final photograph is of the tour with both locomotives at Bridlington (see also page 16).

The July 1961 issue of *Trains Illustrated* reported the line from York to Market Weighton and onwards to Beverley was to have been the first application by BR of Centralised Traffic Control (CTC) to a single line. It involved singling 31½ miles of double track between Bootham Junction, York, and Beverley North signal box; there were to be two extended passing loops, at Pocklington (¾ mile long) and Market Weighton (1¼ miles long). It also included a raft of other measures such as closing seven signal boxes, installing automatic level crossings, and control of many functions from York. But it came to nothing and the line closed instead during November 1965.

Above and opposite page: The Clemens summer family holiday in 1963 was two weeks at Scarborough (14–31 August), although sadly, most of the passenger services were already diesel-worked. But steam still did make regular appearances, and in the first photograph, at the terminus station of Scarborough Central is Ardsley-allocated B1 No. 61030 *Nyala* on a parcels working. The LNER called these locomotives the 'Antelope' class and they were built in quantity after the Second World War. Some 410 were constructed, but only 409 were ever in service at the same time as No. 61057 was written off after an accident in 1950. Very close examination below the shed code of 56B reveals the letters 'SC', indicating a self-cleaning smokebox. In another photograph at Scarborough Central is Doncaster-allocated and soon to be withdrawn V2 No. 60948. This is at the head of an early evening combined parcels/mail plus passenger service at 5.30 p.m. for York and eventually Swindon, where it arrived at 2.18 a.m. the next morning (but not by then with No. 60948).

A station that closed to passenger trains during the middle of our holiday was Scarborough Londesborough Road, seen in the final photograph. By the late 1890s, the excursion platforms at what was then Scarborough station (Scarborough Central after 1933) could not cope with all the summer holiday traffic and there was no room for expansion. The solution was to build this dedicated excursion station on the site of an old engine shed around half-a-mile from the terminus; it was initially called Washbeck Excursion Station, becoming Scarborough Londesborough Road in 1933. This station was used by passenger trains only and never had a freight service. Visible here is part of the 300-yard-long through platform and there was also a bay. Scarborough was famous for its signal gantries and two are visible here plus the steam from a V2 backing to Central station for the 5.30 p.m. departure to Swindon.

These photographs at Malton were taken on the last full day of our summer holiday, Friday, 30 August 1963, but in the antithesis of summer weather. The first, at the twenty-one milepost from York, is looking east: the track on the left goes to the goods depot, straight ahead is the station, and to the right is the engine shed (closed in April 1963). The second shows one of the few steam-worked passenger services, the 4.42 p.m. Fridays only to Whitby with No. 61031 *Reedbuck*. In early 1964, this route's passenger services were said to be losing £49,200 annually and talk was of an autumn closure; this actually happened in March 1965.

Spelling can be a very contentious area, with both the railway companies and the places themselves using different spellings over the years. An example is here at Kirkbymoorside, a small market town in North Yorkshire. Although the town spells itself this way, the NER decided to drop the second 'k' and split the name into two words, Kirby Moorside, then, after Nationalisation, BR changed it to Kirbymoorside.

The railway arrived at Kirbymoorside from Helmsley at the beginning of 1874 and was extended onwards to Pickering in the spring of 1875. But as was the case with many rural railways all over the country, the expansion of road transport after the First World War resulted in a decline in both passenger and freight traffic on the railway. Things did recover during the Second World War but then fell off rapidly. Passenger services (with the exception of excursions and special trains) ceased on and from 2 February 1953. The line onwards to Pickering closed completely at this time; however, a freight service was maintained to Kirbymoorside from Gilling until August 1964. This photograph of J27 No. 65844 shunting in the goods yard dates from 24 August 1961.

The NER's handling of coal traffic has always impressed the author, with 20-ton high capacity railway-owned hopper-type wagons used from 1903, plus the provision of coal 'cells' at stations allowing instantaneous discharge and a much faster wagon turn-round time, often below one day, and the envy of other parts of the country. This can be seen here with the rising track to the left of No. 65844, at the end of which is an elevated coal hopper wagon able to discharge its contents directly into the 'cell' below. (*Ellis James-Robertson*)

In a photograph thought to date from the summer of 1960, this is a view looking to the south-east at Tadcaster and towards Church Fenton. Near the height of the 'Railway Mania' in 1845, the York & North Midland Railway obtained their act for an 18-mile-long line from Church Fenton to Harrogate, and Tadcaster station opened in August 1847. At the time, traffic for London was routed via Normanton and the North Midland Railway; it was hoped the line through Tadcaster would attract business from the Leeds & Thirsk Railway by offering better connections to the south and south-east. Tadcaster station was in the Gothic style, complete with a 44-foot span trainshed. The station buildings were all on the up side and constructed of limestone; this contained the booking office and lobby, second- and first-class waiting rooms, a ladies' waiting room, a coal and lamp room, plus the gents' toilet. The stationmaster's office has a bay window allowing a good view along both platforms in both directions. Great care was taken to provide an equally appealing design for both the exterior and platform elevations. Through the trainshed can be seen the stone goods shed with its pitched slate roof. Despite being a fair-sized town, the railway at Tadcaster involved circuitous journeys to the nearby urban centres of Leeds and York. The result was Tadcaster lost its passenger service in January 1964, but freight continued until the end of November 1966. The local council purchased the station and goods yard sites and obtained permission to redevelop them with warehouses, offices, plus service and light industries. Despite objections, the station was demolished although much of the dressed limestone was reused in a housing development. (*Ellis James-Robertson*)

Another line born of the 'Railway Mania' was the 20½-mile long railway between York and Harrogate. The line was built in stages and the main section from York to Knaresborough was constructed by the East & West Yorkshire Junction Railway. It was one of the few companies that applied successfully to parliament in 1845 and received royal assent in July 1846; the E&WYJR had backing from George Hudson, the 'Railway King'. This station opened on 30 October 1848 as Kirk Hammerton, changing to Hammerton in 1851. On 13 August 1960, a York-bound two-car DMU arrives, of which the leading unit looks to be E50249 (later Class 105). This car rather surprisingly has its own section in the Ian Allan 'ABCs', apparently, it was widely considered to be a replacement for a Metro-Cammell car that suffered irreparable fire damage. Hammerton station is still open with an hourly service to York and Leeds (via Harrogate), although recently work has been done to provide a half-hourly service (introduced during December 2021) and better reliability over the route. This included changes to the track layout, modernised signalling, plus safety measures at some of the level crossings. (*Ellis James-Robertson*)

The 13-mile-long single track branch between Knaresborough and Pilmoor on the East Coast Main Line (ECML) north of York closed to passengers at the beginning of the winter timetable in September 1950. There were three intermediate stations and the first two photographs show Brafferton looking to the east. This had opened in June 1847 on a 5¾-mile-long section from Pilmoor to Boroughbridge, but it would be another twenty-eight years before Boroughbridge became linked by rail to Knaresborough and beyond. Although not visible in these photographs, the signalling was perhaps this line's most unusual feature, and it had been introduced on the branch in the 1930s. There were none of the usual semaphore signals and instead a system of boards was used, some of which could be rotated by 180 degrees; a report refers to one as being of the 'Inn-sign' type. In the centre of the goods yard is a coal hopper wagon on an elevated section of track as described on page 89. Freight carried on to Brafferton from the Knaresborough end until October 1964.

There was another unusual feature to be seen as the branch from Brafferton neared Pilmoor. A spur turned off to the east, crossed the ECML, and joined the line to Gilling and Malton from Pilmoor. This spur never opened and in later years was instead used as a site for enginemen's eyesight tests using the four upper quadrant stop signals in a row seen in the final photograph; these were controlled from the wooden hut in the foreground. All three images date from August 1960. (*Ellis James-Robertson*)

According to Ellis James-Robertson's notes, it is 4.37 p.m. on 16 August 1960 and the location is Alne, just over 11 miles to the north of York on the ECML. A4 No. 60005 *Sir Charles Newton* is in charge of a Kings Cross to Newcastle service and only the month previously had returned from Doncaster works after a 'general' repair including change of boiler. This was repeated in the autumn of 1962 and No. 60005 would end up as one of many A4s that found a final home in Scotland and the three-hour expresses between Aberdeen and Glasgow; it was withdrawn in March 1964. A goods service was maintained to here until August 1964, although passenger services had ceased during May 1958. Evidence of engineering work is visible in Alne's goods yard. The 30 miles of double track line from York towards Northallerton was quadrupled in stages and the first section was to south of Alne from Benningborough following an act of 1894. The final section was the up side from south of Alne to north of Pilmoor; this had recently been finished (the brighter ballast on the furthest track). All this track widening meant problems with the intermediate stations, including replacement or rebuilding; here at Alne, the up platform and Easingwold bay had been demolished. Other improvements included: colour light signalling with three-lens signals, automatic train control (ATC) magnets, concrete cable troughing, and rebuilding overbridges. See also page 14. (*Ellis James-Robertson*)

Two more photographs taken during the early afternoon of 16 August 1960 featuring up services just to the south of Pilmoor, about 5 miles north from Alne in the previous commentary. Ellis James-Robertson kept detailed notes of his black and white photographs, but not so with colour. Also, the colour film was much 'slower' than the monochrome and this can be seen with what appears to be A3 No. 60083 *Sir Hugo*; its number is blurred, this would not have happened with 'faster' black and white film. Thornaby-allocated WD 2-8-0 No. 90593 has charge of a slow-moving train of iron ore tipplers and with no blurring of its number. (*Ellis James-Robertson*)

Continuing our journey down the ECML, the next station north from Pilmoor was Sessay, where these photographs date from 11 August 1960. When additional track was laid at Sessay during the Second World War, it entailed a new down platform, plus also the up was converted to an island. Both show southbound services, although the V2 in the first photograph is unidentified. In the second, WD 2-8-0 No. 90090 is passing through on a mixed freight at 1.25 p.m., another locomotive based at Thornaby. Passenger services at Sessay finished in September 1958, although freight carried on until August 1964. (*Ellis James-Robertson*)

This panorama is looking to the south from the A61 road bridge by Thirsk station on 11 August 1960 at 12.47 p.m. The freight train hauled by V2 No. 60803 on the up slow line can also be seen at the station itself in the introduction on page 15. This locomotive was allocated to the important railway centre of March in East Anglia and had just completed a visit to Darlington works where it had received a 'general' repair plus boiler change; it may well be making its way back to its home depot. Darlington works had responsibility for the entire V2 class between January 1957 and November 1961, even those from as far away as Dundee and Aberdeen. In 1942, an additional down track was laid from north of Thirsk to south of Pilmoor and on the up side from north of Thirsk to north of Pilmoor. Branching to the right is the 1959-closed line to Melmerby, this had been gradually replaced by the section between Northallerton and Melmerby as the latter grew in importance. Thirsk's small engine shed that closed in November 1930 is in the fork between the tracks. In the distance, the bridge crossing the ECML was for the 1848-opened line to Thirsk Town; this was in the centre of Thirsk unlike the station open today that is around 1 mile away. Passenger services at Thirsk Town had finished in 1855 but freight continued until 1966; access was via the Melmerby branch. (*Ellis James-Robertson*)

As we carry on along the ECML, the shadows are lengthening at Otterington on the evening of 10 August 1960. This is the view to the south from the road bridge, and that to the north is in the introduction on page 15. The original station here opened in 1841, straddled either side of the road bridge, but as we have seen already over the last few pages, things changed when the tracks were quadrupled. In the 1890s, powers were obtained for two additional tracks from north of Thirsk to south of Otterington that did not involve alterations to the station. But from 1930–33, much more extensive work was carried out; this included extending the four tracks from south of Otterington northwards to south of Northallerton. Otterington station had to be rebuilt and included a new signal box on the up platform as an unidentified BR Type 2 (later Class 24) heads south on the slow line. The station had lost is passenger service in September 1958, although freight survived until August 1964. Incidentally, the legendary C. J. Allan writing in the April 1961 edition of *Trains Illustrated* regarded the schedule of the Newcastle to Liverpool express seen in the introduction as 'optimistic'. The 44.1 miles from Darlington to York were allowed thirty-six minutes, and this included a section to the south of Thirsk at an average speed greater than the maximum limit for the class. (*Ellis James-Robertson*)

Above and opposite page: Three photographs at Melmerby all taken on the same day, a station that when opened in 1848 was named Wath until 1852. The first line to open here is that branching off to the right in the first photograph. This was the Leeds & Thirsk Railway; it served Harrogate and also provided an alternative route to the north-east from Leeds, joining what is now the ECML at Thirsk. The crossing gates are closed to rail traffic on the line to Thirsk; the tracks appear rusty, and this 6-mile-long railway had closed to all traffic in September 1959. Neville Hill, Leeds-allocated A3 No. 60086 *Gainsborough* has charge of a Liverpool to Newcastle through working just after midday on 15 August 1960; it will join the ECML at Northallerton. The second view is of a southbound DMU at Melmerby station; the track branching off the left is that of the Masham branch. When this branch opened in 1875, Melmerby became a three-way junction. The V-shaped platform the DMU is standing at had also been shared by down Thirsk services. The final photograph is of the goods service for the branch to Masham hauled by D3313; see also page 16. This branch had lost its passenger trains at the beginning of 1931, although freight continued until November 1963. Ahead of D3313 plus also in the DMU photograph can be seen the short platform for Northallerton-bound services; it replaced an earlier one directly opposite the DMU where the Masham track by now joined. The final closure at Melmerby was of the Northallerton line and this happened in March 1967, although it was temporarily reopened for three days in the summer of 1967 due to an accident on the ECML. A freight service for the MOD from the Ripon direction was maintained to a depot about 1½ miles south of Melmerby until October 1969. (*Ellis James-Robertson*)

Some 2¾ miles to the north of Melmerby on the line to Northallerton was Sinderby. This was one of the original stations on the Leeds Northern Railway (renamed from the Leeds & Thirsk Railway in 1851) to Stockton-on-Tees and had opened in June 1852. Initially, there was just a single platform at Sinderby; the second was added when the line was doubled in 1901. On the down platform, this delightful station comprised a two-storey stationmaster's house, a booking office plus waiting room with a hipped roof, and a flat-roofed toilet block; the goods yard was behind these buildings. The up platform had a timber waiting shelter. The date is 16 August 1960 and V2 No. 60947 is passing Sinderby around midday with a southbound train in a view taken from the A1 road bridge. The April 1961 passenger timetable shows only one service per day calling here and that in one direction only, a through train from Darlington to Leeds at 7.28 a.m. (but nothing on Sundays). This ceased at the beginning of 1962 with freight lasting until November 1963; trains continued to pass through the station until the line south from Northallerton closed in 1967. (*Ellis James-Robertson*)

Having spent the last pages travelling northbound over the ECML and the Leeds Northern routes, we finally arrive at Northallerton where the two lines converge, although initially there was no connection between them. A young lad in short trousers (not the author) is clambering over the ECML tracks in a view looking south. D20 4-4-0 No. 62360 is at the head of a special we have seen previously (page 62), the joint SLS and MLS 'Northern Dales' rail tour on Sunday, 4 September 1955. The second photograph was taken in a similar position but on Saturday, 24 August 1963, and shows A4 No. 60016 *Silver Link* with a partially fitted express freight.

Above and opposite page: After filming the Sheffield trams (page 72) on 10 August 1960, Ellis James-Robertson continued his long car journey from North Wales. He arrived here at Northallerton later that same day and when all three photographs were taken. Heading north, D258 is crossing over the A167 at the south end of Northallerton station plus there is a DMU in the bay to the left. The December 1959 issue of *Trains Illustrated* reported the first deliveries of these English Electric Type 4s (later Class 40) to the North Eastern Region had taken place in the October; D237/8. On the ECML they were used on the premier services such as the 'Flying Scotsman', 'Tees-Tyne Pullman', and the 'Master Cutler'; even the overnight express freight service from London to Newcastle. For a while, they became the diesel equivalent of Gresley's pacifics, until the advent of the far more powerful 'Deltics'. The second photograph shows a gradient board relating to the ECML plus the view west from Northallerton station towards the 'Low Level' lines, the old Leeds Northern Railway. This was the location of Northallerton engine shed and prominent is locally allocated K1 No. 62059, although it would soon be transferred to Darlington. In 1966, this locomotive became the very last steam locomotive to be repaired at Cowlairs works, Glasgow. It received a 'heavy casual' repair and left Scotland in September 1966 to take up duties once more in the north-east, but was withdrawn in February 1967. Finally, the view from the north end of Northallerton station with V2 No. 60948 leaving on a Liverpool to Newcastle working. The partially obscured white diamond on the signal post indicates the line is track-circuited. If a train is held here, there is no need to contact the signal box and protect the train (Rule 55) as the signalman will already be aware. Can you make out Ellis's portable reel-to-reel tape recorder at the bottom to the right? Sadly, neither this nor its recordings appear to have survived. (*Ellis James-Robertson*)

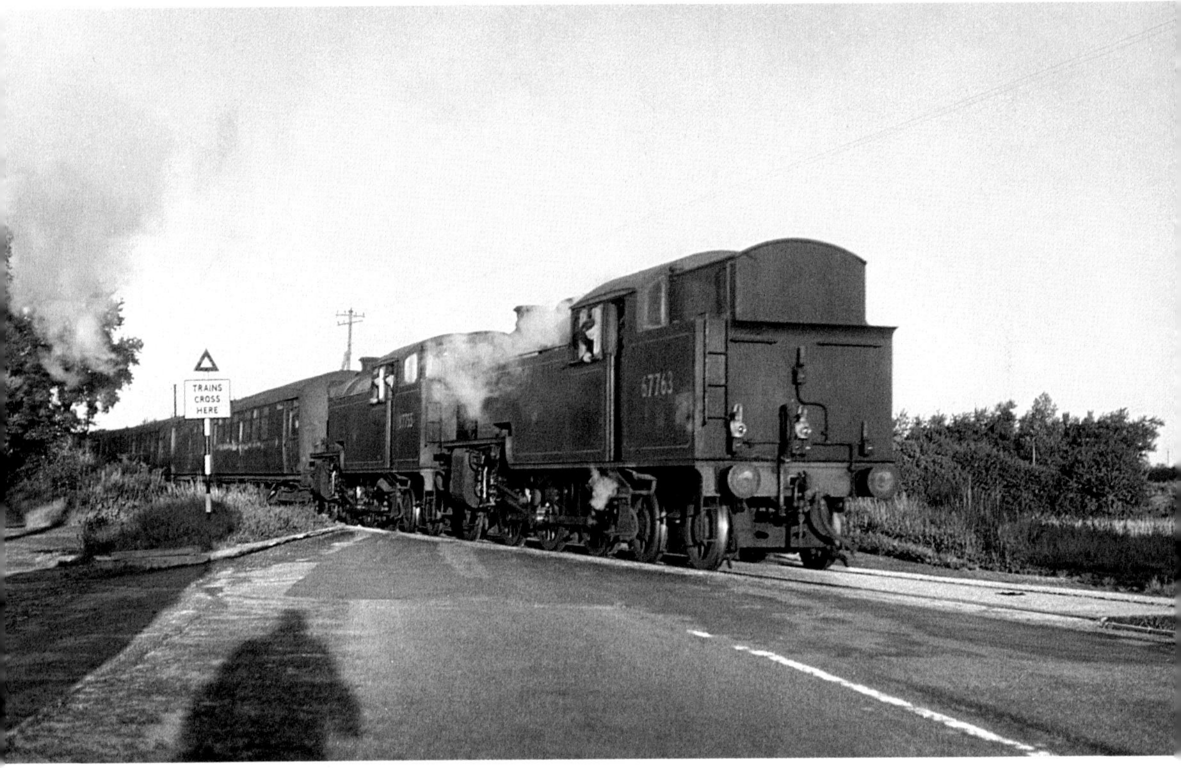
TRAINS
CROSS
HERE
67763

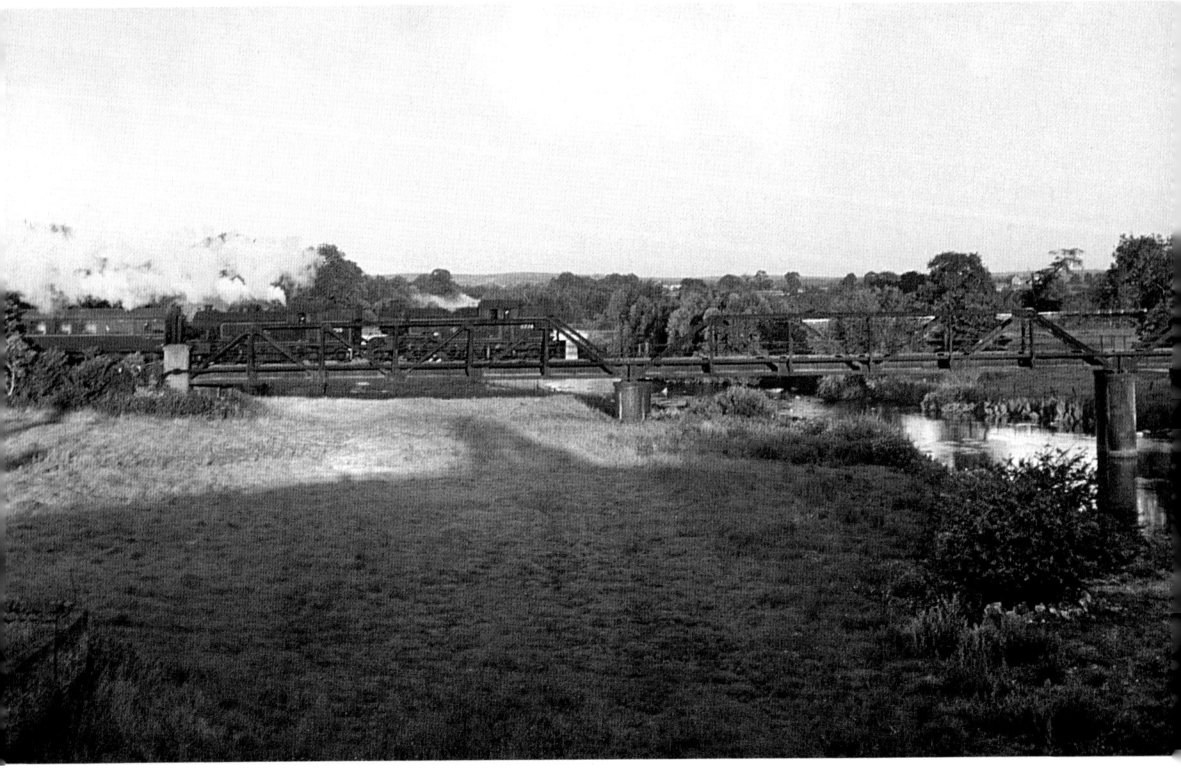

Above and opposite page: Following the outbreak of the First World War, the order was given for construction of the Catterick Garrison; today, it is the largest British Army garrison in the world. A 4-mile steeply graded railway was built connecting the military camp to the 1846-opened Richmond branch of the York & Newcastle Railway. Ellis made an early morning visit to the Catterick area on 15 August 1960 and his shadow is visible in the first photograph as a troop special makes its way back from the camp to Catterick Bridge station on the Richmond line. The locomotives involved are L1 2-6-4Ts Nos 67763 and 67755, both Darlington-allocated. The L1s were the first completely new class of locomotive to appear in Britain after the Second World War, and eventually, 100 were built. A major engineering feature of the Catterick Camp Military Railway was the bridge in the second photograph crossing over the River Swale where this view is looking to the west as the pair pass by. The bridge was built in 1915, originally carried a 2-foot-gauge construction line, and was converted to standard gauge in 1916. The line was run by the military until 1923 when it was handed over to the LNER; services to the camp lasted until 1964. There is little trace left of the Catterick Camp Military Railway nowadays, although this bridge survives and today has as a footpath/bicycle way across it.

The final photograph is at Catterick Bridge station where the military line is joined by a trailing connection, this photograph is looking west towards the terminus of Richmond. We see the first DMU working of the day from Darlington and the time according to Ellis's notes is about 7 a.m. The main station building incorporated the stationmaster's house and waiting room, with a separate timber booking office alongside. The opposite platform had a brick-built waiting shelter and behind the photographer is a level crossing of the Great North Road (A1). Passenger services at Catterick Bridge finished in March 1969 and the freight traffic lasted until February 1970. (*Ellis James-Robertson*)

Above and opposite page: A move north to Darlington, a town with a proud railway history that included the Stockton & Darlington Railway, the earliest public railway in the world to use steam locomotives. The first photograph is taken at the south end of Darlington station in the early summer of 1963. The 1A21 train identification code is believed to refer to the 10.15 a.m. Newcastle to King's Cross, London, and due to depart from Darlington at 11.04 a.m. 'Deltic' D9005 is still unnamed at this time but would be receive the name *The Prince of Wales's Own Regiment of Yorkshire* a few months later.

Darlington North Road works was originally opened for the Stockton and Darlington Railway in 1863, and Alan Maund paid a visit while travelling on the Warwickshire Railway Society's 'Darlington & York' rail tour that ran on a rather foggy 18 January 1964. Works responsibility for the LMR-based 75xxx 4-6-0s had been at Derby, but the last classified steam repair here was in the late summer of 1963 (No. 75042). This responsibility then transferred to Darlington and explains the sight of Croes Newydd-allocated (Wrexham) double chimney No. 75006 at the North Road works; behind is a Q6 plus WD No. 90209. The last steam repair at North Road is believed to have been 'Britannia' 70004 *William Shakespeare* in January 1966 after suffering front end collision damage. The works then closed after removal of plant and machinery later in the year.

Finally, the south end of Darlington station again, but this time on 17 August 1961. According to Ellis's notes, the time is 5.50 p.m. (confirmed by the barely visible clock in the body of the station), so A3 No. 60039 *Sandwich* is likely to be the head of the late afternoon Restaurant Car express from Newcastle to King's Cross, London. This locomotive had returned from a 'general' repair including change of boiler at Doncaster works two months previously, where it also received these trough-style smoke deflectors. (First two photos: *Alan Maund*; final photo: *Ellis James-Robertson*)

Seaham Harbour is about midway between Sunderland and Hartlepool, it had opened in 1831 as an outlet for local collieries owned by the marquis of Londonderry; both photographs here were taken in March 1967. Note the wooden framed chaldron wagon next to the locomotive and, fundamentally, the same as those used around this area in the eighteenth century (a chaldron is an old measure of volume). Two 0-4-0STs numbers are identifiable and both were built locally by Robert Stephenson & Hawthorns Ltd: No. 177 in 1940 (W/N 7036), and No. 183 in 1947 (W/N 7347). Both were purchased second hand from Dorman Long of Middlesbrough in 1963, and both were withdrawn later in 1967.

Moving northwards along the coast from Seaham Harbour, both of these photographs were taken close by Ryhope Junction to the south of Sunderland in March 1967 (see also page 17). No. 90135 in the first photograph and No. 90200 in the second are both War Department (WD) 2-8-0s and both were allocated to Sunderland shed (52G). BR steam came to an end across the entire north-east on 9 September 1967 and Sunderland depot was active until the very end. No. 90135 did survive until September, but No. 90200 succumbed at the beginning of July.

Above and opposite page: Sunderland (South Dock) engine shed had an allocation of twenty-eight steam locomotives at the beginning of 1967, the largest of any shed in the north-east. Fifteen of these were the relatively modern WD 2-8-0s, but a feature here and at other north-eastern depots compared with the rest of the country was the number of Pre-Grouping-designed locomotives still active. Q6 0-8-0 No. 63405 dated from 1919 while inside around the turntable are four J27 0-6-0s, of which three numbers are resolvable: Nos 65880 (1922), 65894 (1923), and 65892 (1923); these photographs were taken on 12 March 1967. Although steam finished in September 1967, the depot remained open for diesels into the 1980s.

112

Above and opposite page: Based in Pallion, Sunderland, since Victorian times, the early history of Doxford's shipyard on the south side of the Wear is rather obscure. It seems to have begun in 1869, later taking over neighbouring yards. Doxford's became famous for the use of crane tanks and visits were made here in both 1968 and 1969. These specialised locomotives have no cables or gears; instead, incorporated in the crane structure is a vertical lifting cylinder whose piston is connected to the end of the jib. A two-cylinder engine is provided to slew the jib through the whole 360 degrees via a large-toothed wheel at the base of the jib pivot. There were three lifting points on the jib allowing 4 tons to be lifted nearest the engine, 3 tons on the intermediate hook, and 2 tons on the outer hook.

0-4-0CT *Southwick* in the first photograph was built by Robert Stephenson & Hawthorns Ltd (RSH) in 1942 (W/N 7069); it was tradition to name these crane tanks after districts of Sunderland. *Roker*, in the second photograph, was one of a pair originally ordered by the New Russia Co. from Hawthorn Leslie of nearby Hebburn in 1918. The order was not fulfilled and the parts were stored until 1940 when they were used by RSH (Hawthorn Leslie's successor) to form *Roker* (W/N 7006) and *Hendon* (W/N 7007). The crane tanks were unusual in having outside Joy valve gear with a correcting lever operated by an eccentric on the driving axle and weighed about 24 tons in working order. Famously, at lunchtime the locomotives could be seen lined up on shed, and at the far end of the row in the final rather smoky photograph is *General* built by Peckett in 1944 (W/N 2049), a conventional 0-4-0ST. The rail operation was replaced by road cranes in early 1971 and the last ship built at Pallion was floated out of the yard in 1989, after which it closed as a shipbuilding yard.

Above and opposite page: A mile or so from Doxford's shipyard on the other side of the Wear was Wearmouth (or Monkwearmouth) colliery. Coal was first won here in 1835 and at the time, it was the deepest in the world (1,578 feet). Eventually, workings extended out on more than one level under the North Sea and reached over 4 miles. 0-6-0T *Jean*, a Hawthorn Leslie product of 1909 (W/N 2769), is seen in both photographs during June 1968; this locomotive spent its entire working life here until scrapped in 1971. Wearmouth was the last deep mine in County Durham and closed in 1993; today, the site is home for the Stadium of Light football ground.

Above and opposite page: For centuries, the north-east was England's main coal-producing area due to its easily accessible seams and navigable rivers. As the eighteenth century progressed, demand increased; this resulted in more pits opening further away from the rivers and the consequent building of waggonways connecting to them. The Bowes family (the same Bowes as Queen Elizabeth the queen mother) plus three other families had decades previously created an alliance. This alliance decided to sink a new colliery at Springwell, about 4 miles south-east of Gateshead and at a height of about 450 feet. They also decided on a new railway down to the Tyne at Jarrow, for which George Stephenson (the 'Father of Railways') became civil engineer. This opened in January 1826 using rope-worked inclines on the steep sections (gravity and powered) plus locomotives on the easier grades (horses initially); by 1855, the line was 15 miles long and had become the Pontop & Jarrow Railway. Springwell Colliery closed in the Great Depression but the company, renamed the Bowes Railway at this time, made significant capital investments and became one of the best-equipped in the area; they guaranteed to ship 1 million tons annually through newly built staithes at Jarrow.

By the time of this June 1968 visit, the line was still busy and in the first photograph, empty wagons have arrived at the top of the gravity-worked Springwell Incline (1¼ miles long at an average grade of 1 in 24). The wagons are uncoupled on the move, pass over the 'kip' (a hump from which the wagons run forward by gravity), and enter Springwell yard. Next is Black Fell Bank Top with its engine house; haulage of loaded wagons uphill at a maximum grade of 1 in 15 took place here. The final view is looking north-east from Black Fell with Mount Moor crossing in the distance; this grade reaches 1 in 13.7 and, as loaded wagons going uphill were involved again, powered from the Blackham's Hill engine house (not visible). Today, there is a museum at Springwell yard and my thanks go to Amanda Cuskin (Outreach Learning and Volunteer Support Officer) for her help.

One of the most interesting industrial lines in the entire country was the Harton Electric Railway that was built to transport coal from collieries in South Tyneside to staithes on the Tyne. The system had been electrified as early as 1908 and was the first such scheme carried out by a colliery company in Britain; the overhead system supplied electricity at 550v DC. There were sharp curves, steep gradients, and very tight clearances. Four-axle electric locomotives could move around double the load of steam and as much of the system was in built-up areas around South Shields, there was the benefit for residents of less noise, smoke, and dirt. All images here date from a March 1970 visit.

First seen are the Harton Low staithes by the River Tyne. Next, note the very low height of No. 15 compared to the wagon; this locomotive was constructed in 1959 by English Electric (W/N 2600). Of the three engines inside the shed by Westoe Colliery, two numbers are resolvable and both were built by Kerr Stuart in 1911: No. 8 (W/N 1203) and No. 7 (W/N 1202). No. 4 in the final photograph by Westoe Colliery was built at the Dynamo works, Stafford, by German company Siemens-Shuckert (generally known as Siemens), and dated from 1909. Another early supplier was AEG (Allgemeine Elektricitäts-Gesellschaft, which translates as 'General Electric Company') as Germany had the experience in this field that Britain did not. The Harton Electric Railway ceased operations in 1989.

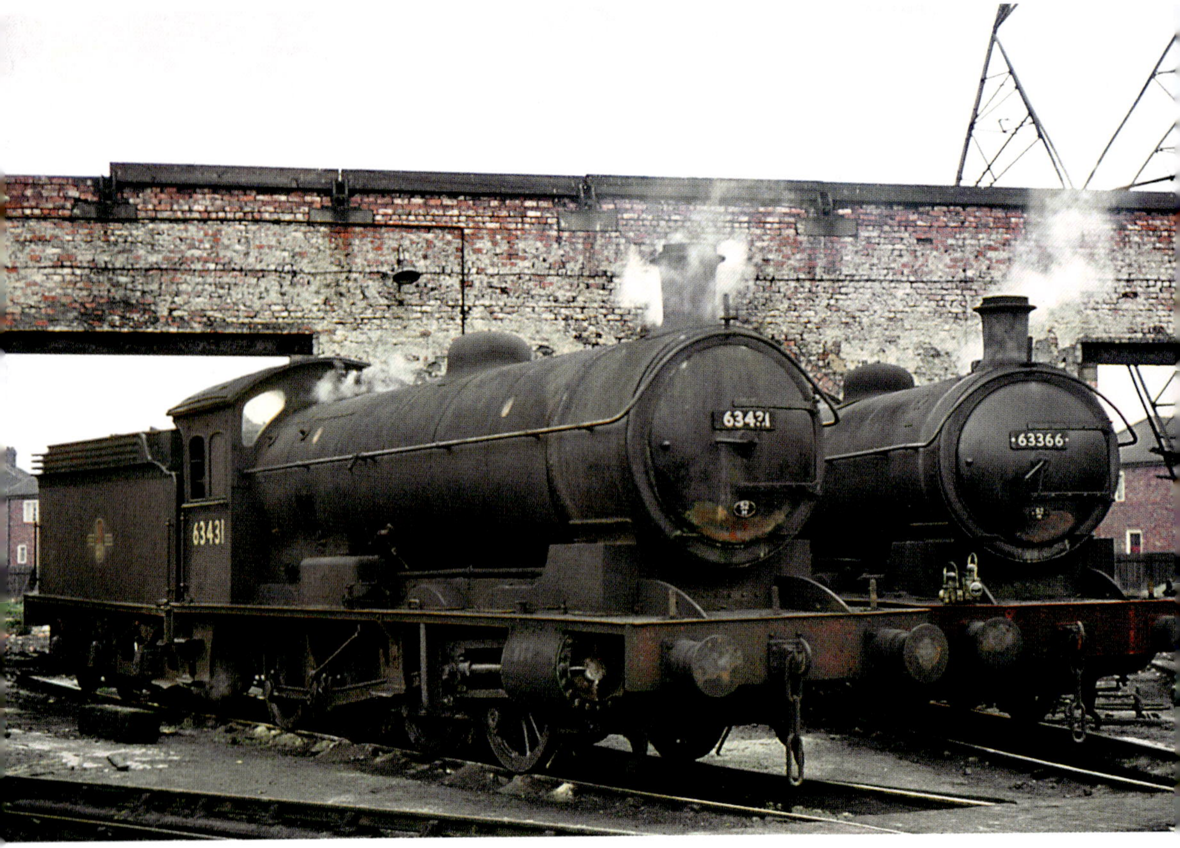

63431
63366
63431

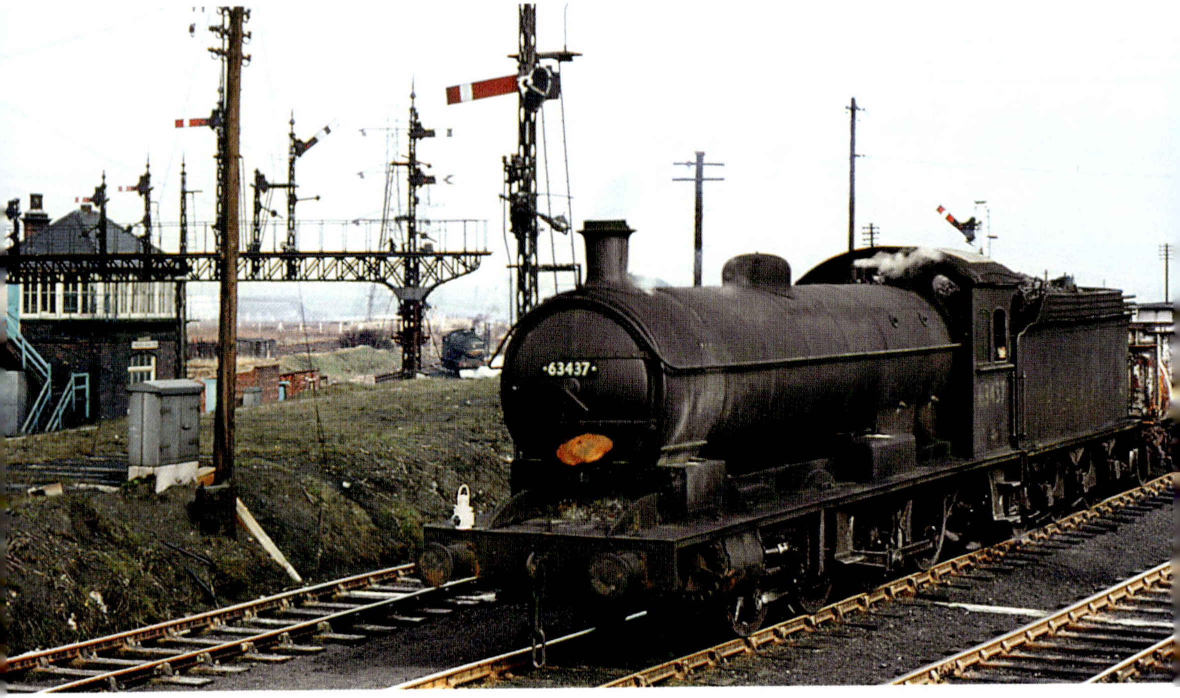

63437

Above and opposite page: Around the beginning of 1966, it was announced that BR steam power in the north-east would last into 1968 (it actually lasted until September 1967). However, Darlington works had ceased steam repairs in January 1966 and to keep the steam stock maintained, including some of the oldest on BR, it was even speculated (incorrectly) that this responsibility would be transferred to Crewe works. As was mentioned on page 110, in relation to BR as a whole, there were significantly more Pre-Grouping-designed locomotives still at work in the north-east than elsewhere. This relates to the Railways Act (or Grouping Act) of 1921 that grouped the existing 100+ railway companies into the 'Big Four'—GWR, SR, LMSR, and LNER. On 1 January 1966, the total BR Pre-Grouping-designed steam locomotive stock was 132, of which eighty were in the north-east; by 1 January 1967, these figures were fifty-one and forty.

All three photographs were taken at or close to Tyne Dock engine shed; the colour views date from 12 March 1967, and the monochrome, Good Friday, 8 April 1966. The 0-8-0 Q6 class was designed for mineral traffic on the NER by Sir Vincent Raven, and 120 were built from 1913–21. Locally allocated Q6s Nos 63431 and 63366 both stand in the open at Tyne Dock's rather dilapidated engine shed. The signal box visible behind Sunderland-allocated Q6 No. 63437 in the second photograph is Tyne Dock Bank Top (see also page 18). At the beginning of 1967, one-third of the entire BR Pre-Grouping-designed steam stock was represented just by the Q6s—seventeen locomotives (Tyne Dock had an allocation of ten). In terms of age, at the other end of design scale were the BR 9F 2-10-0s, where the first had entered service in January 1954. No. 92097 was one of ten allocated to Tyne Dock in the mid-1950s for working trains of bogie iron ore tipplers to Consett ironworks. No. 92097's right hand running board features two air pumps, a modification for Tyne Dock's ten 9F locomotives only; these worked at 85 lb/sq^2 and were used, one for opening and one for closing the discharge doors of the iron ore tipplers.

The author and his father travelled on the joint RCTS and SLS 'Jubilee Requiem' rail tour on 24 October 1964. This was a return journey over the ECML and promoted as 'the last occasion on which an A4 will be allowed to work into or out of King's Cross'. Aberdeen Ferryhill-allocated (61B) A4 No. 60009 *Union of South Africa* was used throughout and is seen on Gateshead shed being serviced before return to London. The impressive smoke effects come from A1 No. 60121 *Silurian* behind No. 60009. To the right and also in the second photograph is V3 2-6-2T No. 67628; this locomotive was withdrawn just one month later.

It is 17 August 1961 and Ellis James-Roberson is at the east end of Newcastle Central station. He noted the time as 4.30 p.m. and that the train is bound for Glasgow. The working timetable for the summer of 1961 lists service 1A22 as the 11 a.m. from London, King's Cross, to Glasgow, Queen Street through train, due to depart from Newcastle at about this time. The locomotive is 'Deltic' D 9006; unnamed in 1961, but during December 1964, it would receive the name *The Fife & Forfar Yeomanry*. The maintenance and performance contract between BR and English Electric for the 'Deltics' (later Class 55) was dated 28 March 1958. It was hoped the first of these legendary locomotives would be delivered one month earlier than contracted, in April 1960. But it was not to be: the first actually entered service in February 1961 with D9006 following on 29 June 1961, and originally allocated to Haymarket, Edinburgh. During early testing of class leader D9000, grave misgivings arose regarding the high noise levels of the 'Deltic' engines, particularly in the drivers' cabs. D9006 was chosen for additional work on noise insulation, but even by the autumn of 1961, the Unions thought noise levels were too high. D9006 was involved with further work during January 1962 and D9015 underwent tests fitted with the modifications. By October 1962, the tests were considered 'satisfactory' and it was hoped to modify all the fleet by May 1963. Individual mileage records for the 'Deltic' fleet were kept until March 1976. At this time, D9006 had amassed 2,534,563 miles (second highest in the fleet, the highest being D9010 with 2,535,411 miles); this works out to approximately 170,000 miles annually. The final working of D9006 was with the 'Night Scotsman' from London to Edinburgh on 4 February 1981 and it was withdrawn on 8 February 1981. (*Ellis James-Robertson*)

Above and opposite page: Another joint RCTS/SLS rail tour was 'The Wansbeck Wanderer' that ran on Saturday, 9 November 1963; the last passenger train to Bellingham and Rothbury. The six-coach train is seen first at Newcastle Central behind No. 43129 ready for a 9.12 a.m. departure. The tour was blessed with fine weather and in the second photograph is being reassembled as it had to be split in two at Rothbury (see page 18). This was to enable No. 43129 to run round its train as it was too long for the turntable at the far end of the station. Final departure from Rothbury was accompanied by music from the local Northumbrian pipe band.

About 5 miles south of Alnwick, Northumberland was Whittle Colliery; it was connected to the ECML by an about 4-mile-long mineral branch. The colliery dated from just after the First World War and at one time was owned by the Co-operative Wholesale Society (CWS). This visit took place during March 1970 and the locomotive visible in both photographs is 'Austerity' 0-6-0ST No. 33. Constructed by the Vulcan Foundry in 1945 (W/N 5306), it went to the Longmoor Military Railway, and in 1946 was sold to Broomhill Collieries, Northumberland. The move to Whittle Colliery was in February 1969, but in 1972, Giesl ejector-equipped No. 33 suffered a piston failure and was scrapped.

The author's father and Ellis James-Robertson travelled together on the SLS and Branch Line Society 'Scottish Rambler No. 2' rail tour on Easter Sunday, 14 April 1963. The first image was taken around midday looking north at Tweedmouth; B1 No. 61324 had worked the tour since departure at 9.30 a.m. from Edinburgh Waverley. The second is at Coldstream looking east where the station was in England despite the town being in Scotland. Visible at the rear of the five-coach special (including a buffet) is Ivatt Class 2 2-6-0 No. 46474; this low axle-load locomotive had just returned the tour from a visit over the weight-restricted branch to Wooler. (*Ellis James-Robertson*)

On 15 August 1960, Ellis James-Robertson made an early morning visit to Catterick Bridge and the one-time Catterick Camp Military Railway (page 104). *The Railways of Northern England in the 1960s* now concludes with this delightful photograph of what Ellis refers to as an 'Old Steam Tar Sprayer' taken on his return south. No location is given in Ellis's notebooks but a clue is the part-visible road sign to the right that says 'RNER'. It seems likely that the right hand turn at the end of this lane is for Scotch Corner and that the main road is the A1. Comparing the view here with Google Street Map, this minor road could be Low Street just over 2 miles to the south of Catterick.

This is a Foden 4½ nominal horsepower, 6-ton 'C' type steam wagon built in 1926 (W/N 12364) with a barely visible number plate of TW 4207 ('TW' is the area code for Chelmsford). It went new to E. Devenish & Sons, Rayleigh, Essex and was used on a contract from the LNER carting manure from stations to market gardens. In 1927, it was sold to A. H. Stutley of Stevenage for £810 and in 1936 was sold again to Tar Roads and converted into a tar sprayer. The years following the First World War were something of a high point for steam wagons, however; by the early 1930s, some manufacturers had gone out of business, and others had switched to internal combustion. The Foden company had its origins in mid-Victorian times but by the early 1930s realised the future lay with diesel, not steam; their first diesel vehicle (the 'F1' model) was made in 1931 and they finished with steam in 1934. By the time of this photograph the owner seems to be D. Wood, Road Contractor, Yeadon, Leeds. Its working life finished with Charrington Hargreaves of Leyburn in 1962 and TW 4207 was then purchased for preservation in 1963 by H. Parkin from Yorkshire. (*Ellis James-Robertson*)